HANDCRAFTS
Without
HEADACHES

MARILYN LASHBROOK

Enjoy Teaching Bible Truths Through Crafts

ISBN 0-86606-425-7

Library of Congress Catalog Card Number 86-61420

Photography, illustrations and layout by Marilyn Lashbrook
Cover Design by Robert Martinez

ROPER PRESS, INC.
Dallas, Texas

TABLE OF CONTENTS

CROSS REFERENCE LIST

Creation	35
Adam and Eve	11, 26
Cain and Abel	23
Noah	13, 60, 63
Abraham	8, 17, 27, 31, 38, 41, 48, 55, 63
Isaac	27
Jacob	8, 47, 66
Joseph	34, 45
Moses	50, 55
Joshua	18, 32, 49
Ruth	41, 45, 59
David	16, 21, 23, 42, 44, 53, 59
Kings	37
Josiah	12, 37, 49, 65
Nehemiah	10, 49
Esther	37, 47
Job	63
Prophets	39, 59
Daniel	10, 16, 21, 23, 28, 30, 42, 65, 67
Jesus	14, 20, 25, 26, 33, 34, 36, 40, 48, 53, 55, 58, 61, 66
Peter	9, 11, 17, 36, 43, 47, 51, 55, 64
Paul	12, 17, 19, 22, 24, 28, 46, 49, 57, 59
Salvation	11, 19, 26, 51, 58
Service	41, 46, 65
Christian Virtues	8, 24, 27, 31, 47, 59, 63
Bible	9, 12, 23, 44
Witnessing	11
Prayer	10, 24

Many of the crafts can be adapted to other stories and themes by changing the verse or motto on the craft.

HANDCRAFTS
WITHOUT HEADACHES

Handcrafts are a wonderful way to reinforce a Bible lesson. And when you know how to prepare, craft time need not be messy or confusing. This book will help you choose crafts appropriate for your class and will guide you in preparation and instruction.

To help you choose crafts, there is a *CODE* at the top of each page that looks like this: 6-8 / 20 / L. The first set of numbers tells you for which ages the craft is suitable. For example, the numbers above indicate that the craft would be best for children 6-8 years of age. The second set of numbers gives an approximate time needed for the craft (20 minutes).

If the craft should be done in two sessions, it would be written as follows 6-8 / 20, 20 / L. The letter at the end indicates whether the cost per student is low, moderate, or high (L = 35¢ or less, M = 36¢ - 75¢, H = 76¢ - $2.00).

Of course, time and cost will be influenced by the size of your class. Small classes may need less time. Supplies will cost less if you buy larger quantities for a big group. You'll soon be able to judge time and cost for your particular class.

MATERIALS are listed on a per child basis to help you determine how much to buy. *GENERAL SUPPLIES* to have on hand are listed as well. Some churches have well-stocked supply rooms, but even so, be sure to check in advance for all of the supplies you need.

One of the most important sections on each craft page is *PREPARATION*. If you follow the instructions under this heading, you will greatly increase your effectiveness as a craft teacher, as well as decreasing the headaches often associated with handcrafts. The preparation section explains what extra preparation is needed when the craft is adapted for young children.

DIRECTIONS are written in the order each step should be completed. Keep them handy when explaining instructions to the children.

Finally, there is a sample *CONVERSATION* under each craft showing one way to help the child understand the relation of the craft to the Bible story and to his life. This may be changed to fit your teaching aim.

Including handcrafts in your schedule need not drive you to the aspirin bottle. When you choose the right craft for your class and prepare it properly, you'll find teaching crafts can be fun and rewarding.

TIPS

PICTURE HANGERS

Make your own hangers for lightweight pictures. Cut card stock or poster board into 1½'' x 3¼'' strips. Fold so that one end is longer than the other. Punch a hole near the fold. To apply picture hanger, place hanger with the long end down against the back of the picture. Place a 2½'' piece of tape across the bottom of the hanger, catching *both* the short and long end under the tape.

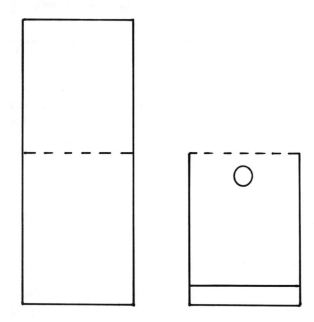

POSTER BOARD PATTERNS

Trace patterns from this book onto poster board and cut out. Children will be able to trace them easily. Patterns can be used again and again, so file them in a pattern file or with the lesson material.

A box of simple shapes will also provide you with ''emergency'' crafts for those days when you have more time than planned. Children may trace and decorate the designs or cut them out. They may glue them to backgrounds or make 3-D slit and slide objects.

FIND A GOOD PRINT SHOP

Call the print shops in your area to find one with a copier that can run card stock and self-stick paper as well as regular bond paper. You can save hours by having patterns xeroxed. And don't forget to ask your printer if he ever has small scraps of paper you could have for children's crafts.

Bible Verses

Print verses for the quarter on 8½'' x 14'' white paper, using a black flair pen. You should be able to fit all 13 verses on the paper. Have one sheet xeroxed per student on self-stick paper. Cut the verses apart and file each week's verse in an envelope. To use, peal away backing and allow child to stick the verse to his handcraft. (My printer charges about 30 cents for a sheet which supplies verses for one child for 3 months.)

Craft Parts

When craft parts are too detailed to trace, xerox them on white or pastel card stock. Children may cut them out and use them as they are. Card stock is slightly more expensive to run than regular bond, but it is worth the cost.

Patterns

Xerox patterns or coloring sheets on plain white bond. Have children scribble the back of the pattern with the side of a pencil point to create a carbon paper effect. By placing the pattern scribbled-side-down and drawing over the lines firmly, the child can transfer the design to the craft material.

PLANNING AHEAD

Purchase inexpensive seasonal items at half-price sales and keep them in your supply closet. Items like Easter egg dye and Easter grass, solid-color foil Christmas wrap, etc. are impossible to buy in July.

Also, collect shells, wheat, acorns, and fall leaves when they are available.

Construction sites often have scrap piles of wood, bricks, and sand. Ask the foreman if you may take leftover materials for children's crafts.

Wallpaper books and pattern books will supply you with plenty of free craft materials. Leave your name and phone number at local shops and ask them to call you when they have old books. Stop in to check occassionally, in case they forget to call. Check with your gardening friends for old seed catalogs, too.

Start a collection of jar lids to use for circle patterns.

KNOWING YOUR STUDENTS

After teaching handcrafts a few times, you will learn what your students are capable of accomplishing. As you plan and prepare, think about your students' abilities. Each group of children is different, but here are a few guidelines:

FOR ALL AGES

Remember, what the child learns about the lesson is more important than how skillfully he completes his craft. Avoid embarrassing the child. Encouragement, support, and acceptance of his work are vital to the child's motivation. Be positive!

FOR NURSERY AND PRESCHOOL

Children under five tend to use too much glue. In preschool classes, it is best to have one glue bottle for the teacher's use only. Don't make exceptions and children will soon learn not to ask. If you must put the glue bottle down for a minute, set it on a high shelf. Otherwise, the chubby hands of a "Glue Bug" will immediately grab it and empty the contents on the table or floor.

FOR ALL AGES

Teach children to clean up after themselves. Younger ones can collect supplies and throw away scraps. Older children should be taught how to clean paint brushes, tables, etc. (Paint brushes should be washed in soapy water and placed bristle-side-up in a can or plastic glass.) Children should learn to take care of supplies and not to waste craft materials.

FOR PRIMARY CHILDREN

Some first graders have been very dependent on mothers or older siblings. These children will ask you to do everything for them. Be available to help, but encourage them to do the work themselves.

FOR ALL AGES

Children will learn to be helpful, considerate, and encouraging to each other as you set the example. Be very aware of the way you treat your students.

FOR NURSERY CHILDREN

Two and three year olds enjoy cutting paper scraps for fun, but they do not have the coordination to cut out craft parts. Do this for them in advance.

FOR ALL AGES

Allow the children to be creative when possible. Often, they will contribute good ideas that you will want to use the next time you teach the craft. Forcing all the children to do a craft exactly alike will stifle their creativity as they grow older. Christian children should learn to stand out from the crowd rather than try to be like everyone else.

FOR NURSERY AND PRESCHOOL

Take away crafts and supplies as soon as young children finish. If you don't, the little ones will destroy their crafts or use supplies to destroy their clothing.

FOR ALL AGES

To avoid discouraging children, try to choose crafts appropriate to the age group. If you wish to do a more difficult craft, be sure to prepare in advance the parts that would be too hard for your students to do themselves. Sometimes a craft may be appropriate for your class, but a less creative child may feel intimidated by the talent of other students. Tracing patterns and rulers will be useful if he does not draw well. Help this child think through the best ways to go about his work.

Knowing your students is important. Consider each child in your class as you plan. Be prepared to help each with his own special needs. Your students will love you for it.

UNSELFISHNESS PLACEMAT

MATERIALS NEEDED PER CHILD

1 large sheet of green construction paper, cut to 11'' x 17''
1 large sheet of pink construction paper
2 12'' x 18'' pieces of clear contact paper

GENERAL SUPPLIES NEEDED

Black Flair pens
Pencils
Rulers
Glue
Poster board pattern of pig (Pages 68 and 69)

ADVANCE PREPARATION

Cut construction paper and contact paper to correct size, one per child. Trace pig pattern onto poster board and cut out. Make a sample of the craft. Have someone help you laminate the place mat with contact paper.

DIRECTIONS

Trace pig pattern onto paper. If you want to make lines for the poem, use a ruler and draw VERY LIGHTLY with a pencil. Write the words in pencil first, then go over them with the marker. Draw on pig's eye, nose, ear and tail with the marker. Cut out pig. Glue to green paper. Ask teacher to help you apply contact paper.

TEACHER: To laminate mats, place contact paper with clear side down on a clean, hard surface. Carefully peal away the backing. Have the child hold one end of the place mat while you hold the other. Hold the mat so that it sags in the middle. Slowly lower the mat until the middle touches the contact paper, then smooth each end downward into the contact paper. Repeat with second side. Seal edges and trim to look neat, but leaving an edge of contact paper all the way around the picture.

CONVERSATION

In our story today, we heard about someone who was very unselfish/selfish. Was that person happy or unhappy. Isn't it strange that when we take everything for ourselves, we are unhappy, but when we give to others, we are happy? When is it hard for you to be unselfish? Sometimes we feel selfish at the table, don't we? Your place mat will help remind you to think of others and not just yourself.

SUGGESTED CAPTIONS

Don't Hog
If You
Love Jesus!

Love is patient,
Love is kind,
It does not seek its own.

8

MEMORY VERSE STRINGER

MATERIALS NEEDED PER CHILD

2   4'' strips of clear contact paper
2   half sheets of construction paper (yellow and orange)
12   multicolor, vinyl coated paper clips

GENERAL SUPPLIES NEEDED

Fine point marking pens, non-permanent
Pencils
Scissors
Paper punch
Poster board tracing pattern   (Page 84)

ADVANCE PREPARATION

Cut enough 4'' wide strips the width of the contact paper roll
for each student to have two strips. Place stack of strips under
several books to flatten them. Trace and cut out several poster
fish shapes from the pattern. Make a sample of the craft.

DIRECTIONS

Trace 2 fish on each color of construction paper and cut them
out. Write one of your memory verses on each fish. Place
contact paper on the table with the clear side down. Loosen
the paper backing at one corner, and carefully pull it off. Place
the fish on the sticky contact paper at least ½'' from each
edge, and at least 1'' from each other. Place the second sheet
of contact paper on the table and remove backing. Pick up by
both ends and turn the sticky side down. Carefully place the
second sheet of contact paper right on top of the one with the
fish on it. Smooth the contact paper down. Now, cut around
the fish, leaving about ¼'' of contact paper sticking out around
all the edges of the fish. Use a paper punch to punch a hole in
the front of the fish.

Fasten 8 of the paper clips together, end to end. Slide a paper
clip through each of the holes in the four fish, then attach the
fish to the stringer with the paper clips. Hang your stringer on a
nail, or tape the top clip to your mirror.

CONVERSATION

When Peter obeyed Jesus, he caught many fish (Jn 21). It is
always best to obey the Lord. When we learn God's Word and
do what it says, we are obeying Jesus. You can learn God's
Word by studying the Bible verses on your fish stringer. Let the
fish remind you of the way Jesus rewarded Peter for obeying.

PRAYER REMINDER

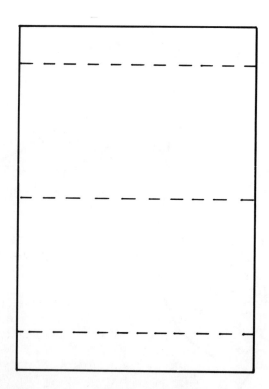

Fold back on all lines.

MATERIALS NEEDED PER CHILD

1   sheet construction paper

GENERAL SUPPLIES NEEDED

Construction paper in variety of colors
Glue
Stapler
Staples
Crayons

ADVANCE PREPARATION

For younger children, fold construction paper before class. Cut out small shapes of construction paper. Write ''I will talk to God'' on one side of the prayer reminder. Make a sample.

DIRECTIONS

Fold your paper in half, then fold about 2'' of each end toward the center. The open end will be the bottom. Write on one side, ''I will talk to God.'' Cut designs from other colors of construction paper and glue to your prayer reminder — it's O.K. if they stick up beyond the top edge. When you have finished designing your craft, open it up like a tent and staple the bottom flaps together. Your prayer reminder will stand on your dresser or dining room table.

CONVERSATION

Why is it important to pray? When should you pray? Sometimes we get so busy we forget to talk to God. It helps to have habits of praying each time we eat and when we get up in the morning and go to bed at night. Your prayer reminder will help you remember to stop and talk to God.

GOSPEL STORY BOARD

6-12 / 30 / L

MATERIALS NEEDED PER CHILD

1   4'' x 8'' piece of corrugated cardboard
1   6'' x 10'' piece of flannel
1   no. 10 envelope

GENERAL SUPPLIES NEEDED

Blue, black, red, white, yellow felt, cut in 3'' squares
Masking tape
Scissors
Marking pens
Poster board patterns (page 81)

ADVANCE PREPARATION

Cut cardboard, flannel and felt to designate sizes. Trace patterns onto poster board and cut out. Make a sample.

DIRECTIONS

Center the cardboard on the flannel. Trim corners from the flannel even with the tips of the cardboard. Wrap flannel flaps up over the cardboard and tape in place with masking tape. Place in the envelope with your name on it.

Trace and cut out felt shapes. Store shapes in the envelope with the flannel board. Use the flannel set to tell your friends about God's way for us to be saved.

CONVERSATION

[Use flannel set to explain the Gospel]

Black heart - The Bible says our hearts are full of sin and darkness. We cannot live in God's beautiful Heaven with our sin.

Red cross - That's why Jesus died on the cross. He washed away our sin with His own blood.

White heart - If we believe in the Lord Jesus to save us from sin, He will make our hearts clean and fill them with His light and love.

Yellow smile - When we know God has forgiven our sins, we can be happy inside. We can be happy that we will live in Heaven. We can be happy that Jesus is our Friend and God is our Father. We can be happy that God's Spirit comes into our lives to help us learn to do the things that please God and make us the kind of people we should be.

Blue question - Would you like to ask Jesus to forgive your sins and give you new life? You can pray and tell Him so right now.

BIBLE STUDY NOTEBOOK

MATERIALS NEEDED PER CHILD

1   duotang folder

GENERAL SUPPLIES NEEDED

Construction paper
Plasti-tak
Tempera paint
Pencils
Scissors
Toothbrushes
Plastic knives
Newspaper
Poster pattern for Bible shape
Felt tip pens

ADVANCE PREPARATION

Trace Bible shape onto poster board and cut out. Make a sample of the craft. (Pattern on page 96)

DIRECTIONS

Trace the Bible shape onto construction paper and cut it out. Use plasti-tak to fasten it lightly to the front of the folder. Place the folder on newpaper. Dip a toothbrush in paint and tap off the excess on the side of the paint jar. Hold the toothbrush above the notebook and scrape with the plastic knife to make tiny drops of paint spatter all over the front of the folder. After the folder is completely dry, remove the construction paper Bible shape and save the plasti-tak.

Use felt tip pens to write inside the Bible shape, "MY BIBLE STUDY NOTEBOOK." Write your name inside your folder. Put several sheets of notebook paper inside.

CONVERSATION

It is important for Christians to study the Bible. You can use your notebook to make notes each day of the verses you read and any questions you have. Write down things to pray about and mark them off when God answers your prayers. Keep your notebook with your Bible so you'll remember to use it. You might even want to bring your notebook to church on Sundays so you can write down what you learn in Sunday school and church.

Dip toothbrush in paint, then scrape bristles with a knife.

RAINBOW MOBILE

MATERIALS NEEDED PER CHILD

½ sheet of white poster board (14'' x 22'')
1 wire coat hanger

GENERAL SUPPLIES NEEDED

White thread
Watercolor paints (8-color pans, Crayola brand recommended)
Large watercolor brushes
Pencils
Patterns from pages 82-83
Scissors
White glue
White glitter
Permanent black markers, fine and wide points
Paper punch

ADVANCE PREPARATION

Cut posterboards in half. Cover painting tables with newspaper. Make patterns out of poster board. Cut out enough patterns to have one for every 5 children in your class. Mix white glue with a little water to thin it down. Decide how much of the craft you will do during each craft period. Obtain a long, low box for glitter.

DIRECTIONS

Trace the patterns onto your poster. Make one rainbow, one sunshine, and four raindrops. Cut out the shapes and write your name in pencil on the back of each shape. After you cut out all of the shapes, use the pattern again to trace the holes. Punch them out with a hole punch.

Paint stripes on your rainbow in the following order: red at the top, then orange, yellow, green, blue, purple. Paint the sunshine and the raindrops. Set everything aside to dry and help clean up the tables, wash your brush and put away the supplies.

When the pieces are dry, draw faces on the sunshine and the raindrops with markers. Quickly and lightly, brush the glue mixture over your rainbow. Do not scrub the brush back and forth or the paint will run. Do not try to cover the whole rainbow; little spaces will not matter. While the glue is still wet, place your rainbow over the glitter box and sprinkle it with white glitter. Shake off the extra glitter into the box. Set aside your rainbow to dry. Help clear the tables and wash out the brushes.

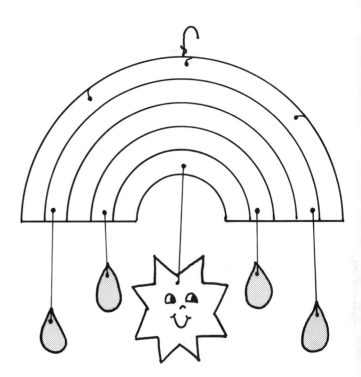

Place your rainbow over a coat hanger. Push a piece of thread through each hole and tie a knot around the wire to hold the rainbow in place. Repeat with each of the top holes. Tie a longer piece of thread to the sunshine and to each raindrop. Tie the sunshine to the center hole in the bottom of the rainbow. Tie each of the raindrops to one of the other holes.

Wrap finished crafts in a sheet of newspaper and fasten with masking tape. This will prevent tangling of mobile parts on the way home.

CONVERSATION

What did the rainbow mean to Noah (Gen 9)? God has promised us many things. What promises will you remember when you look at your rainbow?

ADAPTING FOR PRESCHOOL OR PRIMARY CHILDREN

If you have a small class and have the time to pre-cut all the pieces before class and tie the crafts together after class, preschool and primary children will enjoy painting the rainbows. If you wish, you may simplify the craft by eliminating the hanger and mobile parts, simply painting a rainbow and adding the glitter. Or trace the pattern onto large sheets of manilla or white construction paper and allow the children to paint or glue on 1'' squares of colored construction paper.

JESUS IN THE MANGER

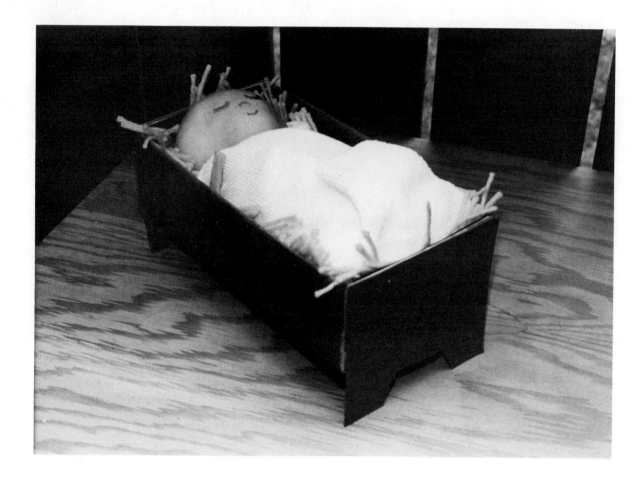

ADVANCE PREPARATION

Cut flannel into 12'' squares. Cut button thread into 6'' lengths, two per child. Trace the pattern for the end of the manger on corrugated cardboard and cut out two for each child. Cut 2 of every 3 sheets of construction paper to measure 9'' x 9½''. Save the scraps and cut to 2½'' x 4¼'' (two per child). Make a sample of the craft.

DIRECTIONS

Snip top of kleenex box at an angle to all 4 corners as shown in the illustration. Fold down flaps and staple in place. Fit one piece of construction paper inside box on the long side, then fold paper out around outside of box, creasing at folds. Remove paper and apply glue to side of box, inside and out. Replace paper and hold in place for a minute. Repeat the same with the other side of the box. Glue bottom flaps in place and hold together with a piece of tape, if needed. Glue one of the small rectangles to each end of the inside of the box.

Trace the two cardboard ends on brown construction paper. Cut out the brown paper and glue one piece to each of the cardboard ends. Glue the uncovered side of the ends to the short ends of the kleenex box. Hold in place with clothespins, standing manger on end until glue is dry.

Make a 4'' round ball of fiberfil and stuff it tightly into the toe of the nylon stocking. Make a 4'' x 6'' roll of fiberfil and stuff into the stocking, pressing it against the 4'' ball. Use a piece of button thread to tie off the head from the body. Tie tightly, using several knots. Use a second piece of thread to tie off the bottom of the doll. Trim away all but about ½'' of the excess nylon band.

Wrap the baby in flannel. Place straw or grass into the manger and lay the baby on top.

CONVERSATION

Jesus left His home in Heaven to come to earth as a little baby. Mary wrapped Him in cloth. She did not have pretty baby clothes for Him. What do you think it was like to sleep in a bed of hay? Mary and Joseph were poor, but Jesus' birth was very special. God put an unusual star in the sky to guide the wisemen to the place Jesus lived. Angels sang and told shepherds about the wonderful child who had been born. Jesus was not just any baby. He was the Son of God.

MATERIALS NEEDED PER CHILD

1 knee-high nylon stocking
1 Kleenex box (175 count size)
1 12'' square of white flannel
3 sheets of brown construction paper
4 clothespins per child

GENERAL SUPPLIES NEEDED

Corrugated cardboard
Tacky glue
Black, felt-tip laundry marker
Button thread
Fiber fil stuffing
Pattern from page 95
Scissors
Stapler
Staples
Straw or dried grass

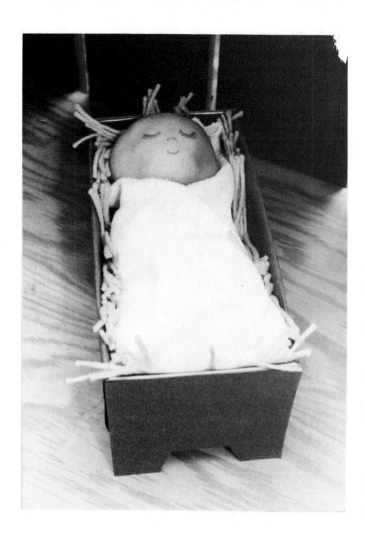

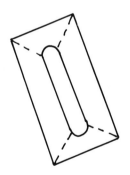 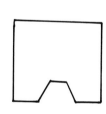 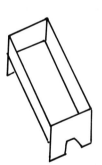  

Clip Kleenex box from opening to each corner.

Trace pattern for end of manger. Make two of cardboard and two of construction paper.

Cut two and tape together at center.

Staple cardboard ends to Kleenex box. Glue on brown paper according to directions.

Stuff fiber fil into nylon knee high stocking and tie off head with button thread. Tie off bottom with button thread, then trim away excess nylon.

LION SOCK BANK

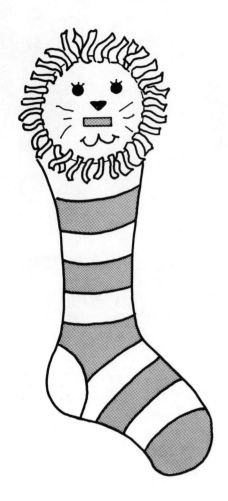

MATERIALS NEEDED PER CHILD

1   lid and band for wide mouth canning jar
1   sock

GENERAL SUPPLIES NEEDED

Yellow poster board
X-acto knife for teacher's use only
Black paint marker
Brown yarn, cut in 2'' lengths
Tacky glue

ADVANCE PREPARATION

Trace canning jar inner lid on yellow poster, one for each student. Use an X-acto knife to cut slots for coins in the yellow circles. [Work over several layers of cardboard to protect work surface.] Cut yarn into 2'' lengths, or buy pre-cut rug yarn. Draw lion faces on the lids with paint marker. Make a sample of the craft.

DIRECTIONS

Glue the lion's face in the lid band. Glue sock around the jar lid. Put glue on the top edge of the jar lid about ¼ of the way around the lid. Stick pieces of yarn in the glue to look like a lion's mane. Continue adding glue and yarn until the mane goes all the way around.

CONVERSATION

I have a hungry lion here, but he won't hurt you. In fact, he will help you save money. You can feed him with pennies and nickels and dimes. Pretty soon he will be a fat lion and you can open him up and take the money to the bank or use it to buy something special.

Daniel was thrown into a den of real lions, and they were hungry! But the lion's did not hurt him. Why not? Have you ever been afraid to do the right thing? Have you ever been afraid to pray in front of others? What can we learn from Daniel?

Glue poster lion face inside canning jar ring [pattern for face on page 75].

BIBLE WORD BANNER

MATERIALS NEEDED PER CHILD

1   18'' dowel stick
1   piece felt, 17'' x 17''
1   piece twine, 24'' long
1   pattern for words (Page 90)

GENERAL SUPPLIES NEEDED

Sheets of felt in assorted colors
Straight pins
Tacky glue
Needles, large
Thread

ADVANCE PREPARATION

Cut dowel sticks to proper length. Cut felt to correct size. Xerox word patterns one per child. Cut twine. Make a sample.

DIRECTIONS

Fold the felt over the dowel stick and sew it in place. Tie the ends of the string to the ends of your dowel stick and put a small drop of glue where the string joins the stick to hold it in place.

Cut out the pattern letters and designs. Pin them to small sheets of felt and cut out. Arrange letters and designs where you want them on the front of your banner. Glue them in place.

CONVERSATION

Many of the stories in the Bible can be summed up with the words "Trust" and "Obey." How did the main character in today's story learn the importance of trusting and obeying what God said? How does God tell you what He wants you to do? What are some things the Bible tells you to do? You're banner will remind you to trust what God says and to obey His Word.

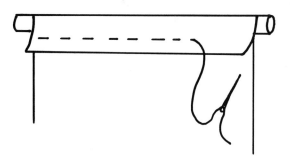

Fold top of felt over dowel and sew in place.

Tie twine to dowel, then secure with a drop of glue.

17

SUNSHINE DESIGN IN FRAME

MATERIALS NEEDED PER CHILD

2 sheets of white poster board (11'' x 14'')
1 compass
1 ruler
1 sheet of solid-color wallpaper from sample book
1 picture hanger (See page 6)

GENERAL SUPPLIES NEEDED

Bright paints or markers
Art brushes if paint is used
Pencils
Round plates and jar lids to trace
Scissors
Rubber cement
Masking tape
Poster pattern, 9'' x 12'' rectangle

ADVANCE PREPARATION

Cut posters. Cut one 9'' x 12'' poster pattern. Tear out sheets from wallpaper book. Make a sample.

DIRECTIONS

Picture:

Design an interesting sunshine design using the compass, ruler and lids. It can be as simple or detailed as you like. Use bright markers or paint to color in the spaces. Put your name on one corner of your picture and set aside.

Frame:

Center the poster pattern on your poster board and trace around it. Use the point of your scissors to punch a hole in the center of your poster. Cut to the pencil line, then cut all the way around the pencil line. Keep the outside frame and throw away the center part.

Choose your wallpaper and turn it up-side-down on the table. Paint your frame with rubber cement, then turn it over and center it on the wallpaper. Use a ruler to measure 1½'' all the way around the frame on the inside and the outside and make a pencil line on the wallpaper. Cut on the pencil line. Now, trim away the outside corners at an angle. Then, cut a straight line from the inside corner of the wallpaper to the inside corner of the poster board. Fold over the inside wallpaper flaps and glue down with rubber cement. If needed, use masking tape to hold them in place until the glue dries. Turn your sunshine picture up-side-down and center over the poster frame. Fold over the outside wallpaper flaps and glue to the back of your picture. Tape in place with masking tape until dry. Tape a picture hanger on the back of the picture. Turn over and admire your work.

CONVERSATION

Sunshine is mentioned many times in the Bible. It is mentioned in the creation story and in the story of Jonah and in the story of Joshua. In the story of Jesus' death, the sun was darkened to show what a terrible thing people had done to God's Son, Jesus. But the sun did not stay dark because Jesus did not stay dead. He came back to life and went to live with God in Heaven. When we see the sunshine, we can feel happy inside because Jesus is alive and He gives life to us.

KITE WALL DECORATION

SUNSHINE DESIGN IN FRAME

Cut away corners of wallpaper and fold flaps to back of frame.

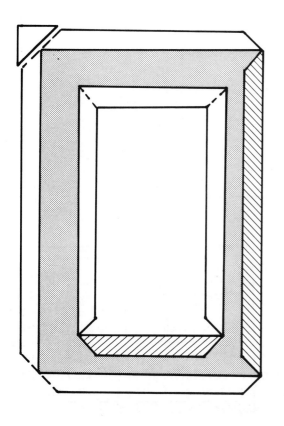

MATERIALS NEEDED PER CHILD

1 sheet pastel colored construction paper
1 piece of yarn, 18'' long

GENERAL SUPPLIES NEEDED

Construction paper scraps, assorted pastel colors
Crayons
Tape
Poster board kite patterns (Page 87)

ADVANCE PREPARATION

Trace kite pattern and bow pattern onto poster board several times and cut out. Cut an 18'' length of yarn for each student. Make a sample of the craft.

DIRECTIONS

Trace kite pattern onto construction paper and cut out. Draw a picture on the kite of something that flys through the sky. It can be a living thing or a machine. Trace 3 bows and cut out. Tie the bows at three different places on the yarn, leaving the top end free. Tape the top end of the yarn to the bottom end of the kite on the back. Write your name on your kite.

CONVERSATION

Have you ever wished you could fly? It must be a wonderful feeling of freedom to rise up into the wind and look down at the earth. But we don't have to fly to feel free. The Bible says in Isaiah 40:31 that when we serve the Lord, He will give us strength. What does it mean to serve the Lord? With God's help we can feel strong like the eagles that soar through the air. What kind of flying thing would remind you of the freedom and strength God gives?

19

GOSPEL BOOKLET

MATERIALS NEEDED PER CHILD

1   sheet 9'' x 12'' black construction paper
1   sheet 8'' x 11'' white construction paper
1   piece of blue ribbon, 10'' long
1   red construction paper cross   (Page 84)

GENERAL SUPPLIES NEEDED

Gold paint pen — fine point
Black marker — fine point
Tape
Glue stick

ADVANCE PREPARATION

Trace cross pattern onto poster board and cut out. Cut white paper and ribbons to proper size. For younger children, write the verse on the white paper and the caption of the front of the craft. Make a sample craft.

DIRECTIONS

Fold the black paper in half. Fold the white paper in half. Open both sheets. Tape ribbon to the black paper near the fold as shown in the illustration. Glue the white paper inside the black paper so the fold matches at the top and bottom. Glue the cross to the right side of the white paper. Write John 3:16 on the left half of the white paper. Place the ribbon in the fold of your craft and close the booklet. On the front cover, print "The Bible tells me . . . " with the paint pen.

CONVERSATION

The Bible answers a very important question for us. That question is, "Why did Jesus die?" Do you know the answer to that question? Let's read the verse on the craft and talk about what it says to us.

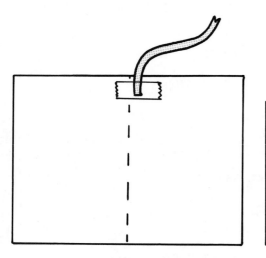

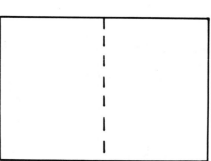

AUTOGRAPH HOUND

MATERIALS NEEDED PER CHILD

⅓   sheet of poster board (22'' x 9'') light colors
2   xerox sheets — both parts of dog pattern (Pgs. 72-73)

GENERAL SUPPLIES NEEDED

Pencils
Black Flair pens
Glue
Scissors
Brown or black felt
Colorful fabric scraps and trims
Black or dark blue glitter
Paper clips
Staight pins

ADVANCE PREPARATION

Xerox pattern. Cut poster boards to correct size. Make a sample craft.

DIRECTIONS

Scribble the back of the pattern with the side of the pencil point. (Tip: Hold the paper backwards against the window and scribble over the lines only.) Paperclip the pattern with the scribbled side down on the poster board. Trace over the lines of the pattern, pressing hard enough to transfer the picture to the poster board. When you have drawn all lines, remove the pattern and go over the lines on the poster with a black Flair pen. Save the pattern.

Cut the dog's ear and collar from the paper pattern. Pin the ear pattern to felt and cut it out. Glue the felt to the poster. Pin the collar pattern to fabric and cut it out. Glue the fabric collar to the poster. Spread a small amount of glue on the dog's eye and sprinkle with glitter. Shake off excess glitter into a box or over a folded paper. Write the Bible verse at the top of the dog's back. If you like, cut out the dog.

CONVERSATION

We learn from the Bible that it is very important to have good friends. Our friends should be people who love God and obey the Bible. In order to have good friends, we must learn to be good friends to others. How should friends treat each other? What should friends do when they disagree? It's fun to collect autographs from friends. You can have your friends sign their names and phone numbers on your happy hound. When you need a friend, you'll know who to call. And you can use your autograph hound as a reminder to pray for each of your friends during the week.

JOY BREAD DOUGH PLAQUE

MATERIALS NEEDED PER CHILD

1   4'' piece of light wire
1   pattern to look at (Page 85)
1   piece of aluminum foil, about 8'' x 11''

GENERAL SUPPLIES NEEDED

Bread dough made from recipe below
Pencils, toothpicks, plastic knives
Acrylic tube paints
Clear nail polish, any brand
Art brushes, small and medium
Baking sheets
Access to an oven

ADVANCE PREPARATION

Make arrangements to use oven at church or bring crafts home. Prepare dough the morning you plan to teach, keeping it in a plastic bag, in a tightly covered container. Tear off aluminum foil sheets. Bring baking sheets to class. Make a sample of the craft.

DIRECTIONS

First Day:

Shape letters from bread dough on top of aluminum foil. Press down so the letters run together. Use pencil to make the hole in the ''O.'' Fold center of wire around a pencil and twist to form a loop. Slide the loop off of the pencil and spread the ends apart. Insert the ends of the wire into the ''J'' and the ''Y'' before baking. Write your name on the foil with a toothpick or pencil. Carefully lift your foil and place it on a baking sheet.

TEACHER: Bake dough for 1-2 hours in a 250-300 degree oven.

Second Day:

Paint baked dough with acrylic paints. Let each coat dry before adding decorative designs. Set aside to dry. Help clean up tables and wash paint brushes thoroughly.

Third Day:

Paint the back of the baked dough with a layer of clear nail polish. Wait 5 minutes, then add a second coat. Wait 5 minutes, then turn over and paint front and sides with a coat of clear nail polish. Wait 5 minutes and add another coat. Set aside to dry.

CONVERSATION

Joy is an interesting word. What does it mean to you? Many Bible people had joy, even though they had problems. Where does joy come from? Let's read Phil. 4:4 from the Bible. What does that verse tell us about joy? Is joy something that happens to us, or is it something we do in obedience to God? When you feel like complaining, what can you do to have joy? Hang your craft in your room to remind you that God wants you to be joyful in every situation.

RECIPE:

Mix together:
2 cups flour
1 cup salt
1 cup water

PSALM 119:11 OBJECT LESSON

MATERIALS NEEDED PER CHILD

1   sheet red construction paper
1   xeroxed Bible with Psalm 119:11 (page 76)
2   pieces of yarn, 18'' long

GENERAL SUPPLIES NEEDED

Tape
Paper punch
Crayons
Pencils
Scissors

ADVANCE PREPARATION

Trace heart pattern onto poster board and cut out. Cut yarn in 18'' lengths (2 per child) and wrap tip with small piece of tape. Xerox one Bible for each child. Make a sample of the craft.

DIRECTIONS

Trace the heart pattern onto red construction paper 2 times. Cut out the hearts and hold together. Punch holes along both sides of the hearts, but not the top. Tie yarn to the top hole on one side and lace to bottom hole. Tie yarn. Repeat on other side. Use crayons to decorate heart and write your name. Cut out the Bible and place in the heart through opening at the top.

CONVERSATION

[Read Ps 119:11 from the Bible.] How can we hide God's Word in our own hearts? How will that help us not to sin? Psalm 119:11 would be a good verse to memorize, wouldn't it? And your craft will be a good place for you to save your other memory verse papers.

THANKFULNESS DIARY

MATERIALS NEEDED PER CHILD

1   church bulletin with color photo, cut in half
7   pieces of white bond paper, 5½'' x 8½''
1   piece of yarn, 24'' long, both ends taped

GENERAL SUPPLIES NEEDED

Felt tip pens
Hole punches
Tape

ADVANCE PREPARATION

Cut paper and church bulletins. Tape both ends of the yarn pieces with cellophane tape for easier lacing. Make a sample craft.

DIRECTIONS

Place 7 sheets of paper between the front and back of the bulletin. Punch a hole about 1½'' from the top, one the same distance from the bottom and one in the middle along the left side of the booklet. You may need to separate the paper into 2 stacks to punch it more easily.

Turn the stack of paper up-side-down. Lace one end of the yarn through the top hole and the other end through the bottom hole. Turn over the booklet and pull the yarn through.

Even up the ends. Push one end through the middle hole, wrap it around the back piece of yarn, then push it up through the hole again. Tie a knot with the 2 ends of yarn. Tie a bow. Write your name on the front cover of the booklet. If there's room, write, "My Thankfulness Notebook."

CONVERSATION

Sometimes we take good things for granted and forget to say "thank you" to God, our parents, teachers, and friends. Why is it important to show our appreciation for what people do for us? How does it help others when you are thankful? How does it help your attitude when you are appreciative?

You can use your thankfulness notebook to develop a good habit. Each day, before you go to bed, ask your mom to help you make a list of good things that others have done for you that day. Also, make a list of things God has blessed you with. When you say your prayers, thank God for His blessings and for the people who care about you. The next day, find each person on your list and say "thank you!" for what they did for you the day before. Be sure to thank your Mom too! Before you go to bed, check off all the people on your list that you thanked, then make a new list. Before long, you will find yourself saying "Thank you!" right away when people do special things for you. And you might even begin to thank God for things all through the day. Just think how happy you will be when you learn to enjoy and appreciate God's blessings all day long!

JESUS DESK PLAQUE

MATERIALS NEEDED PER CHILD

2   6'' x 7'' pieces of yellow poster
1   xerox copy of the pattern (Page 81)
12   craft sticks

GENERAL SUPPLIES NEEDED

Tacky glue
Black tempera paint
Small felt tip pens, black
Pencils
Art brushes, small and medium

DIRECTIONS

Turn the pattern so the picture is face down on the table. Scribble with the side of the pencil point over the entire sheet. Place the pattern, scribbled-side down over a piece of yellow poster board. Hold firmly in place while tracing over the lines of the pattern. Press hard enough with the pencil to transfer the lines to the poster. Remove the pattern when you've traced over all the lines.

Use a felt tip marker to darken all the lines on the yellow poster. Paint around the lighthouse and the letters with black paint. [Work from left to right, top to bottom if you are righthanded.] Be careful not to drag your hand through the wet paint. Set aside to dry.

Glue 6 craft sticks into a stack. Make a second stack of 6 sticks. Set aside to dry.

Glue a second piece of poster to the back of the one you painted. Set aside to dry.

Glue one stack of sticks to the bottom, front edge of the plaque. Hold in place until dry. Glue the second stack to the bottom, back edge of the plaque. Do not stand the plaque up for several hours.

CONVERSATION

How is Jesus like a lighthouse? What are two ways Jesus helped the man in our story to see (Jn 9)? How can Jesus help you see?

Scribble back of pattern.

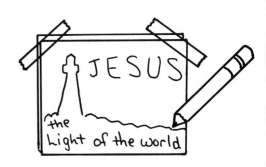

Tape pattern over poster and trace lines, pressing firmly.

SALVATION OBJECT LESSON CRAFT

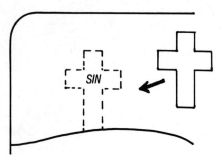

Glue cross over the word "SIN."

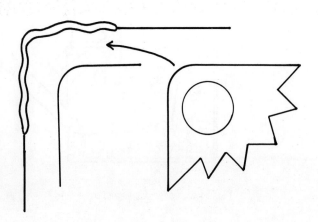

Glue sun to upper border of box.

MATERIALS NEEDED PER CHILD

½ of a MacDonald's sandwich box - neatly trimmed
1 each of pre-cut paper parts (Older children can trace parts and cut them out)
1 pre-punched paper hanger

GENERAL SUPPLIES NEEDED

Glue
Construction paper (light blue, purple, green, yellow, orange, gray or lavendar)
Scissors
Patterns from page 95
Pencils

ADVANCE PREPARATION

If you have a small class, trace the patterns on the specified color construction paper and cut out enough for each child. Write the word "sin" on the blue background where shown on the pattern. If you have a large class, trace the patterns onto separate ditto masters and run through a duplicator on various colors of construction paper (clean duplicator wick when you finish). If you teach children 6 or older, trace each pattern several times on poster board and cut out for the children to use as tracing patterns. Make a sample of the craft.

DIRECTIONS

Write name on back of box. Glue red cross over the word "sin." Glue purple hills at bottom of blue paper. Glue this piece into the box. Glue orange center into yellow sun. Put a small amount of glue on the upper edge of the box corner. Glue sun in place. Put a small amount of glue on the lower edge of the box. Glue grass and tomb in place.

CONVERSATION

We have all done wrong things like disobeying, lying, and hating others. God calls those things sin. We cannot go to Heaven with our sin. When Jesus died on the cross, He covered up our sin with His own blood. When we believe in Jesus as our Savior, we are saved from sin. God gives us eternal life in Heaven.

MATERIALS NEEDED PER CHILD

¼ sheet red poster board (11'' x 14'')
2 black chenille wires, cut in half
8 brass fasteners
3 yards white yarn
2 3'' x 9'' pieces of white construction paper
1 black construction paper spider body (from pattern on page 75)
2 4mm wiggle eyes

GENERAL SUPPLIES NEEDED

Masking tape
Glue stick
Black permanent marker - medium point

ADVANCE PREPARATION

Cut poster, yarn and construction paper. Cut out 1 black spider body per child. If desired, print caption on white paper and xerox one copy per child. Make a sample.

DIRECTIONS

Print the caption on the white paper. Glue the white paper to the bottom part of the red poster. Press 8 brass fasteners through the poster at the top at uneven intervals. Turn the poster over and press the fasteners apart. Place a piece of masking tape over the prongs, taping them down to the poster. On the front, tie one end of the yarn to a brass fastener. Wind the yarn back and forth around the fasteners, pulling the yarn tight enough to hold, but not tight enough to bend the poster. After you criss-cross the poster about 10 times, loop the yarn around the outside of the brads to outline the spider web. Leave a little extra yarn at the last fastener so you can unwind it later and play with it. Cut off most of the extra yarn.

Wind the 4 pieces of chenille wires together at the middle and spread out the legs. Bend legs down a little so spider will stand up. Bend feet upward a little so they will hook under the yarn web. Glue eyes to the spider's head. Glue the spider's body to the center of the chenille wire legs. When the spider is dry, slide 2 or 3 of its feet under the yarn web. Write your name on your craft.

CONVERSATION

Do you know what happens when you tell a lie? Pretty soon, you tell another and another and another. Each lie leads to more lies. Pretty soon, you get caught. Lies are like a sticky spider web. Once you get caught, it's very hard to get out. If someone lied to you, would you want to believe that person again? Do you think people will want to believe you if you lie to them? God knows lies will hurt us and the people we love. That's why He tells us in the Bible that we should not lie to each other. The next time you are tempted to tell a lie, remember what God says in the Bible. Don't get caught in a web of lies!

SPIDER WEB STRINGING TOY

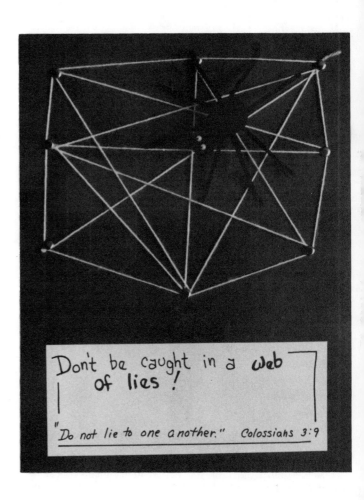

Don't be caught in a web of lies !

"Do not lie to one another." Colossians 3:9

T-SHIRT

MATERIALS NEEDED PER CHILD

1   T-shirt
1   xeroxed pattern (from pages 77-80)
1   black, ball-point, laundry marker

GENERAL SUPPLIES NEEDED

Masking tape
Iron
Ironing surface
Small art brushes
One of the following:
    Fabric paint
    Puff paint
    Glitter paint
    Crayons (excluding true red and black)
If crayons are used, you will also need:
    Vinegar-water mixture
    Paper towels

ADVANCE PREPARATION

Decide which type of color to use. Xerox a pattern for each child, plus a few extras. Use simpler patterns for younger children. After the first class, buy T-shirts in boy's or men's sizes. It's best to buy shirts several sizes larger than the child wears since they will shrink. Some children will also prefer shirts that are extra baggy. Make a sample to wear to class the first day.

DIRECTIONS

Day 1

Show children your shirt and explain how the shirt is made. Take children's sizes. If you decide to let them choose a pattern, have one child take orders for the copier. Talk about how the shirts can be used to tell others about the Lord.

Day 2

Try on the T-shirt to make sure it fits. If so, print your name or initials on the inside of the collar with a laundry marker. Place pattern inside shirt so picture shows through front of shirt. Straighten the pattern and tape it in place with masking tape. Tape the shirt to the table. Use a laundry marker to trace over the lines of the pattern. This will be easier if you use the thumb and forefinger of one hand to hold the fabric while you make short marks with the laundry marker. Leave the pattern inside the shirt to absorb excess paint or crayon.

Day 3

Use paints or crayons to color the design on your T-shirt.

Day 4

Finish painting or coloring your shirt.

Day 5

If you painted your shirt with fabric paint or glitter paint, you may take it to the girl's or boy's dressing room to change into your shirt. If you used puff-paint, ask the teacher to use an iron or blow dryer to puff the paint according to directions on the paint package. If you used crayons, take your shirt to the teacher to be ironed.

TEACHER: Mix ½ cup vinegar to one gallon water. Spread out one shirt at a time on the ironing surface. Soak a paper towel in the liquid and squeeze out excess. Open up towel and place on top of the crayon design, covering it completely. Press with hot iron until paper towel dries. DO NOT MOVE IRON BACK AND FORTH OR DESIGN MAY SMEAR. Lift iron and set it down squarely to dry entire towel. (The vinegar makes color permanent while the heat pulls out the wax.)

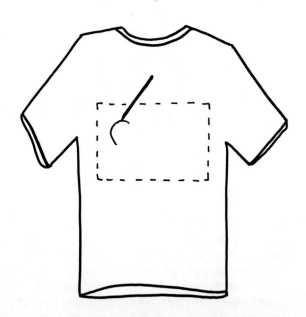

*Place pattern inside shirt and trace lines
with a laundry marker.*

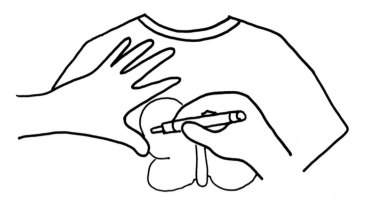

Stretch fabric slightly as you color or paint.

Dip paper towel in diluted vinegar solution.

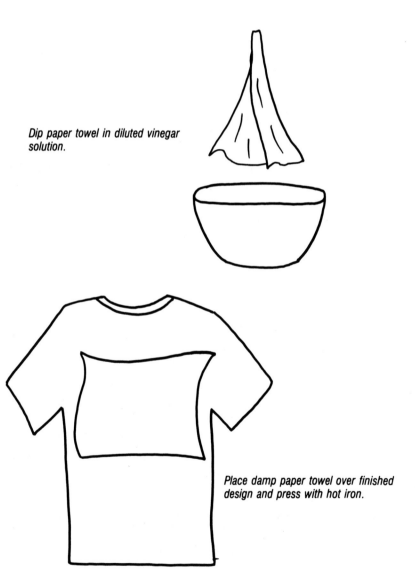

Place damp paper towel over finished design and press with hot iron.

BOOKSHELF

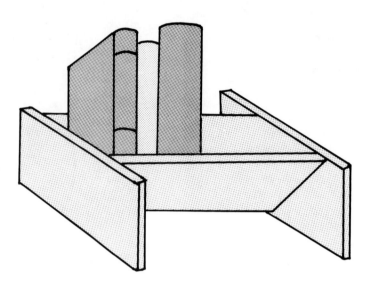

MATERIALS NEEDED PER CHILD

2   7'' pieces of 1'' x 6'' plywood
2   10'' pieces of 1'' x 6'' plywood

GENERAL SUPPLIES NEEDED

Sandpaper
Hammers
Nails (4 penny)
Latex enamel paints
1'' paint brushes
Paint pens
Lots of newpaper
Wood glue

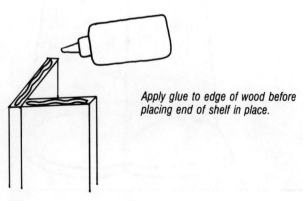

Apply glue to edge of wood before placing end of shelf in place.

ADVANCE PREPARATION

Have wood cut to correct size. Make a sample of the craft.

DIRECTIONS

Working over newspaper, sand rough edges of wood until smooth. Carefully fold up newspapers and throw away. Glue one of the long boards to the other long board at right angles to form a ''V'' shape. Nail together with four nails. Apply wood glue to one end of the v-shaped shelf. Glue to a small board so that the top of the ''V'' touches the top of the small board (see illustration). Repeat with the other end. Be sure your shelf is level, then nail each end with 3 nails, one at each point of the ''V''.

Paint bottom of shelf with enamel paint. Dry overnight. Paint top of shelf. Dry overnight. Use paint pens to decorate and personalize your bookshelf.

CONVERSATION

What does the Bible mean to you? How has it helped you? Do you know where your Bible is right now? Sometimes our Bibles are lost because we don't have a special place to keep them. Books are our friends, and the Bible is the best book of all. It deserves a special place in our hearts and in our homes. The bookrack you make will give you a place to keep your Bible where it will not get lost or torn or dirty.

DOOR KNOB HANGER

MATERIALS NEEDED PER CHILD

1   poster board door hanger (Page 92)

GENERAL SUPPLIES NEEDED

Book of names with Christian meanings
Felt tip pens
Stickers
Scrap paper
Pencils

ADVANCE PREPARATION

Trace door hanger. Cut one for each student from light blue,
yellow or pink poster board. Make a sample of the craft.

DIRECTIONS

Look up your name in the name book and write down the
meaning on scrap paper. Print your name lightly in pencil at the
top of the door hanger in large letters. Underneath, print the
meaning of your name in smaller letters. Go over the pencil
letters with a felt tip pen. Decorate the door hanger with
drawings or stickers.

CONVERSATION

In Bible days, names were very important. People knew the
meaning of their names and tried to live up to them. Your
name is special. Knowing what your name means will give you
something to live up to.

PAPER TRUMPET

MATERIALS NEEDED PER CHILD

2   sheets of heavy yellow construction paper
1   piece of yarn, 20 inches long

GENERAL SUPPLIES NEEDED

Poster board trumpet pattern (page 92)
Tape
Crayons
Pencils
Scissors

ADVANCE PREPARATION

Trace trumpet pattern onto poster board and cut out. Cut yarn into 20'' lengths. For nursery children, cut out 2 trumpet pieces in advance. Make a sample.

DIRECTIONS

Roll one piece of yellow construction paper to make a roll about 1¼'' in diameter. Fold a piece of tape over at each end and tape twice along the loose edge. Trace the trumpet pattern twice on the second sheet of paper and cut out. Use crayons to decorate. Tape the two trumpet parts into place on opposite sides of roll. Punch a hole through the tape on each side at the mouth piece. Tie one end of the yarn through each hole.

CONVERSATION

Who blew trumpets in our Bible story (Jud 7)? Why did they blow the trumpets? What happened? What will happen if we obey and do what God tells us to do?

WISE MEN STICKER PICTURE

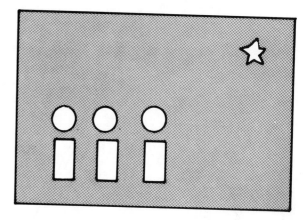

2-5 / 10 / M

Roll one sheet of construction paper and tape middle and ends.

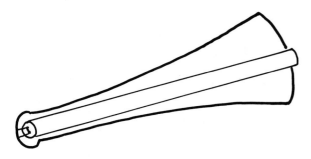

Tape roll to one of the trumpet pieces.

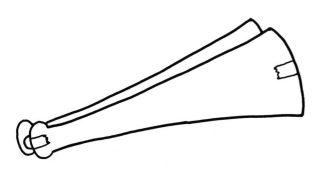

Tape second trumpet piece on opposite side of roll.

MATERIALS NEEDED PER CHILD

1   sheet of dark blue or black construction paper

GENERAL SUPPLIES NEEDED

Self-stick stars
Self-stick large round dots
Self-stick rectangular stickers
1 bright yellow paint pen

ADVANCE PREPARATION

Use the paint pen to write across the bottom of each sheet of construction paper the words, ''They saw His star in the East.'' Make a sample.

DIRECTIONS

Use dots and rectangles to make wisemen at the bottom of the page. Place a star in the sky.

CONVERSATION

The wise men came to look for Jesus. What does it mean to be wise? People who are wise want to know Jesus. People who are wise study the Bible to learn about God. We learn about the Bible and Jesus when we come to (church, VBS, Christian school, etc.).

CLAY MANGER SCENE

9-12 / 30, 30 / M-H

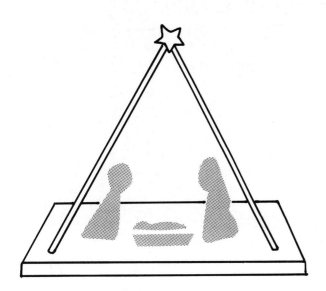

MATERIALS NEEDED PER CHILD

1   piece of scrap lumber (approx. 4'' x 6'')
1   piece of corrugated cardboard (approx. 1'' x 9'')
1   gold foil star
1   piece of sandpaper

GENERAL SUPPLIES NEEDED

Mexican Pottery Clay (or other self-hardening clay)
Tacky glue
Newspaper
Waxed paper

DIRECTIONS

Make small clay figures of Mary, Joseph, Jesus, and the manger and place on waxed paper to dry overnight.

Sand edges of wood until smooth. Fold cardboard in half and glue to wood like an up-side-down "V" shape. Glue a star to the top point. Glue dried clay figures in place on the wood.

CONVERSATION

What was different about the day Jesus was born from the day you were born? What was the same? Do you think your parents were eager to share the good news with other people? In what way did God show His desire to share His joy with others?

JOSEPH'S COAT

2-7 / 15 / L

MATERIALS NEEDED PER CHILD

1   xerox copy of page 91

GENERAL SUPPLIES NEEDED

Scraps of brightly colored fabric and ribbon
White glue
Scissors (older children only)
Crayons

ADVANCE PREPARATION

Take pattern to the print shop or church office to have copies made. Cut fabric into small strips for younger children.

DIRECTIONS

Glue fabric strips to Joseph's coat. Color Joseph's face and hands if desired.

CONVERSATION

How did Joseph's father show how much he loved his son (Gen 37)? Do you ever make things for people you love? God is our Heavenly Father. He made many beautiful things to show how much He loves us. We can be glad we have a God who loves us so much.

TISSUE AND WAXED PAPER PICTURES

MATERIALS NEEDED PER CHILD

1 9'' x 12'' sheet black construction paper
2 8'' x 11'' pieces waxed paper

GENERAL SUPPLIES NEEDED

1 package (assorted colors) tissue paper
Scissors
Pencils
Iron
Ironing board or plywood

ADVANCE PREPARATION

Cut sheets of waxed paper to the specified size. Unfold package of tissue paper and cut into 4'' x 5'' stacks (or smaller if you have a large class).

DIRECTIONS

Fold black construction paper in half to form a 6'' x 9'' rectangle. Use a ruler to draw a pencil line 1½'' from the sides of the paper, except for the folded edge. Cut along this line and open the outer part to form an aquarium (save middle pieces for another craft). Set aquarium frame aside.

Stack about 6 small sheets of tissue paper together. Draw a simple fish shape on the top sheet. Cut on your line through all thicknesses of paper. Throw away the top piece with the pencil marks on it. If you like, make another stack of tissue and cut out water plants.

Arrange shapes on one sheet of waxed paper, being sure to leave some of the waxed paper showing between the shapes. This is important. After you have your fish arranged, carefully lower a second sheet of waxed paper on top. Lift the whole craft gently from the table and walk slowly to the ironing table where the teacher will seal your picture for you. [NOTE TO TEACHER: It only takes a quick swipe over the entire picture to seal the waxed paper. If you iron it too long, the wax will melt away and the paper won't stick together.]

Fit the fish picture behind the opening in the black paper. Tape in place. Turn the picture over and hold it up to the light. You may want to hang your picture in a window in the classroom or at home.

CONVERSATION

God created many kinds of fish. Do you remember which day He made them (Gen 1)? What else did He do that day? Why do you think God made fish?

MANY-LAYERED KEY CHAIN

MATERIALS NEEDED PER CHILD

30 3'' x 4'' pieces of construction paper, assorted colors
1   poster board pattern
1   pencil
1   pair of scissors
1   key chain
1   styrofoam vegetable tray with name on it for storage
1   piece of sandpaper or an emery board

GENERAL SUPPLIES NEEDED

White glue, diluted slightly with water
Small paint brushes
Clear nail polish
Paper punches

ADVANCE PREPARATION

Cut construction paper into 3'' x 4'' pieces. Trace patterns onto poster board, one for each child. Cut out poster patterns and punch hole at top. Make a sample.

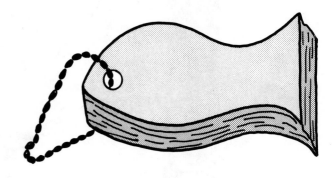

(Pattern on page 85)

DIRECTIONS

Trace the poster pattern (including the hole) onto 10 pieces of construction paper. Place 2 blank sheets of construction paper under a piece with the pattern traced on it. Cut and punch all 3 sheets at one time. Continue until all 30 are finished.

Brush the diluted glue onto one construction paper piece and glue on a second piece of a different color. Continue until all 30 pieces are glued together. Allow to dry overnight.

When dry, sand the edges with sand paper or an emery board until smooth. If you sand the edges on an angle, the colors will show up better.

Paint the top and sides of your craft with clear nail polish and wait until the polish dries. When dry, paint the back with polish. If you like, add more coats of polish, but allow each coat to dry before adding more.

Fasten chain through hole.

CONVERSATION

There are many different Christian symbols. What is the value of a symbol? When are symbols worthless? How can we avoid allowing our symbols to lose their value?

Brush each piece with diluted glue and stack while glue is wet.

CROWN

Tape parts of crown pattern together.

Crown pattern on page 88

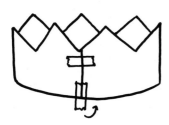

MATERIALS NEEDED PER CHILD

1   strip yellow poster board, 24'' x 5''

GENERAL SUPPLIES NEEDED

Stars
Stickers
Sequins
Tacky glue
Crayons
Tape

ADVANCE PREPARATION

Trace crown pattern onto poster board doubling the length, and cut out. Trace and cut one crown for each child. Make a sample.

DIRECTIONS

Decorate your crown with stars, stickers, and sequins. Use crayons to draw designs if you like. Ask the teacher to put your name on the back. Wait until the glue dries before wearing your crown.

TEACHER: Measure child's head and tape crown to correct size.

CONVERSATION

Who wears a crown? Do you remember the name of the king (or queen) in our Bible story? Jesus is the King of Kings. That means His children are princes and princesses. If God is your Heavenly Father, you are part of a royal family. When we get to Heaven, God will reward us with beautiful crowns for the good things we have done.

MEMO PAD

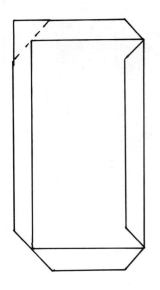

Clip corners before folding wallpaper to back.

God will not forget His Promises.

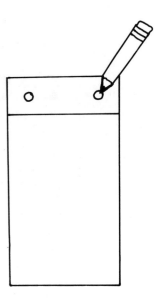

Trace holes from small piece onto large piece and punch.

GENERAL SUPPLIES NEEDED

Rubber cement
Scissors
Paper punch
Fine point markers
Cellophane tape

MATERIALS NEEDED PER CHILD

1   4'' x 7'' piece of poster board
1   4'' x 1½'' piece of poster board
1   5'' x 8'' piece of wallpaper
1   5'' x 2½'' piece of wallpaper
10 sheets of 4'' x 5½'' memo paper
1   12'' length of yarn
1   1'' x 3'' piece of construction paper

ADVANCE PREPARATION

Cut posterboard, wallpaper, memo paper, construction paper, and yarn to correct size. Wrap ends of yarn with small piece of tape. Make a sample of the craft.

DIRECTIONS

Cover one side of the larger poster board with rubber cement, then center the poster, glue-side-down on the back of the larger sheet of wallpaper. Repeat steps above with smaller piece of poster board and wallpaper. Trim off all corners at an angle. Fold wallpaper flaps to the back of poster pieces and rub your fingernail over the folds to flatten them. Glue the flaps in place and press down until they dry. On the smaller piece, measure 1'' in from each side and ¾'' down from the top and draw 2 dots. Punch the holes. Mark holes on the stack of memo paper and punch. Stack the paper on top of the large poster piece (wallpaper side up). Place the small poster piece on top of the paper. Thread the yarn through the holes and tie it in a bow. Write on the piece of construction paper, ''God Will Not Forget His Promises.'' Glue construction paper to poster piece, below the memo paper.

CONVERSATION

How did God show his faithfulness to the people in our Bible story? How does He show his faithfulness to us? You and I need to write things down sometimes or we will forget. That's why we need memo pads. But God never forgets. He will remember His promises to you.

NEW LIFE PLANTER

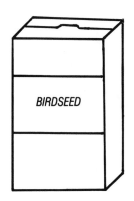

MATERIALS NEEDED PER CHILD

1   styrofoam cup
1   waterproof marker
1   plastic bag with twist tie

GENERAL SUPPLIES NEEDED

Potting soil
Birdseed
Water

ADVANCE PREPARATION

Make a sample.

DIRECTIONS

Draw a face on the cup with a marker. Fill the cup with potting soil. Sprinkle the top of the soil with birdseed. Water gently. Place your craft in a plastic bag and close with twist tie.

OPTION: For VBS, place cups in warm, light place at the beginning of the week and keep soil moist. By the end of the week children will see growth. Place in plastic bags to send crafts home with children.

CONVERSATION

Have you ever wondered how plants can grow from tiny, little seeds? It is God who gives life to the seeds and makes them grow. God gives life to all the plants and animals and people in the world. What happened that brought death into the world? Sin causes death, but Jesus died to wash your sins away. He wants to give you new life, if you will receive Him.

LIGHT SWITCH COVER

MATERIALS NEEDED PER CHILD

1   light switch cover — brown or tan
1   small art brush

GENERAL SUPPLIES NEEDED

Acrylic paints
Dish soap
Paper towels
A small paint pen (optional)
Masking tape

ADVANCE PREPARATION

Unwrap covers and place all screws in a box so they won't be lost. Make a sample craft.

DIRECTIONS

Wash light switch covers in soapy water, rinse, and dry completely. Paint a sunshine design in the center and write the verse at the top and bottom. If you would rather think up your own illustration for the verse, that is fine. Set aside to dry. Before taking your craft home, tape screws to the back with masking tape.

CONVERSATION

Do you ever remember a time when you were afraid of the dark? It is not much fun when the lights go out, is it? How is sin like the darkness? How does Jesus bring light into our lives? What would the earth be like if there was no light? Is there light in Hell? Is there any darkness in Heaven? What does a person have to believe to be saved from sin and given life in Heaven?

MAP PLAQUE

MATERIALS NEEDED PER CHILD

1   9'' x 12'' piece of cardboard
1   9'' x 12'' piece of construction paper
1   4'' x 10'' piece of a colorful map
2   large, colorful buttons

GENERAL SUPPLIES NEEDED

Pattern for car, from page 70
Construction paper scraps
Glue
Black flair pens
Pencils
Scissors

ADVANCE PREPARATION

Cut a colorful map into 4'' x 10'' strips. Trace a car pattern onto poster board and cut out. Remove buttons from cards. Make a sample of the craft. For younger children, cut out enough construction paper cars for each student to have one.

DIRECTIONS

Glue the construction paper to the cardboard. Glue the map to the top of the picture, centered from side to side. Write your name on the back of the craft. Trace the car onto a scrap of construction paper and cut out. Glue car at the bottom of the picture to one side. Glue on 2 buttons for wheels. Write "I Will Go Where God Leads Me" on the construction paper.

CONVERSATION

Who are some Bible people who went wherever God told them to go? Can you think of a Bible person who did not go where God sent him? Is it better to go where God says or to go where you want to go? Why? Who knows what is best for you?

LION'S FACE

MATERIALS NEEDED PER CHILD

1   yellow paper plate
1   orange lion muzzle and 2 ears (from pattern on page 70)
2   black eyes (from pattern on page 70   )

GENERAL SUPPLIES NEEDED

Bright orange yarn, cut into 2'' lengths, or pre-cut rug yarn
White glue
Pencil
Black marker
Paper punch

ADVANCE PREPARATION

Cut yarn into 2'' lengths. Trace muzzle pattern onto orange paper and outline with black marker — one muzzle for each child. For younger children, cut out muzzles in advance. Trace ear pattern on orange paper and eye pattern on black paper — two per child.Make a sample a sample of the craft.

DIRECTIONS

Put your name on the back of the plate. Glue the muzzle to the front of the plate in the middle. Glue on the eyes above the muzzle. Squirt a little bit of glue on the edge of the plate, about 2'' long. Place pieces of yarn in the glue so they stick out like a lion's mane. Use about 2'' more glue and continue adding yarn and glue until the entire plate edge is covered. Glue on ears.

CONVERSATION

Why did the king have Daniel thrown into the lion's den (Dan 6)? What did the king think the lions would do to Daniel? Why didn't the lions hurt Daniel? Did Daniel believe God would help him? Do you believe God will help you when you are in danger? You do not need to be afraid to do what is right. That's always the best thing to do. Do the right thing, believing God will watch over you.

SEASHORE COLLAGE

MATERIALS NEEDED PER CHILD

1   rectangular cake cardboard
1   piece of white netting, cut 2'' longer and wider than cardboard

GENERAL SUPPLIES NEEDED

Shells
Sand, available as sandbox sand or builder's sand
Blue, green, white tempera paints
Cotton
Assorted construction paper
Scissors
Pencils
White glue
Dried flowers
Felt tip pens
Masking tape
Art brushes
Old margarine cups and jar lids for mixing paint
Clean tin cans for water
Newspaper for tables

ADVANCE PREPARATION

Cut netting to proper size. Make a sample. Line a box with a garbage bag, then add sand.

DIRECTIONS

Put your name on the back of the cardboard. Paint the water and sky. Allow the paint to dry. Apply glue to the area where you want sand, then take your cardboard to the sand box and sprinkle sand on the glued area only. Shake off the excess sand. Add shells, flowers, clouds, seagulls, fish, etc. as you like.

Center the finished picture up-side-down on top of the netting. Wrap the edges of the net to the back of the picture and tape with small bits of masking tape to hold in place, then use large strips of tape to hold the edges of the net firmly in place.

CONVERSATION

Have you ever walked along the seashore picking up shells and listening to the waves rolling up on the sand? The shore can be a peaceful place. Maybe that's why Peter went there after Jesus died (Jn 21). What do you think Peter was remembering? How do you think he felt? Why do you think he wanted to go fishing? Can you imagine how excited he must have been to see Jesus? Do you think Peter wanted to show Jesus how much he loved Him? What did Jesus ask Peter to do? What does that mean? How can you show your love for Jesus?

MEMORY VERSE SCROLL

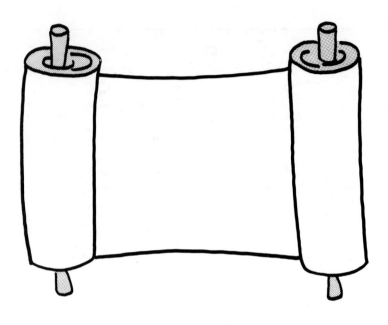

MATERIALS NEEDED PER CHILD

2 dowel sticks or straws cut to 6½''
1 piece of white paper, 4¼'' x 11''
1 toilet paper roll
1 piece wrapping paper, 4½'' x 6''

GENERAL SUPPLIES NEEDED

Tacky glue
Tape
Pencils
Bible

ADVANCE PREPARATION

Cut white paper and wrapping paper. Cut dowels or straws to 6½'' length. Make a sample of the craft.

DIRECTIONS

Look up the memory verse and write it on white paper. Glue dowels or straws to sides of the verse paper. Set aside to dry. Cover the cardboard roll with wrapping paper and tape in place. Wrap a piece of tape over each end of the roll to keep the paper from slipping off.

When glue is dry on the scroll, roll it from each end and place it in the cardboard roll.

CONVERSATION

At one time, the Bible was written on scrolls because people had no printing presses or equipment to make books. Men called scribes printed every letter of the Bible books by hand on long scrolls. The scribes were very careful not to make mistakes because they knew how important God's Word was. We learn Bible verses because they will help us remember to obey God. David wrote in the Bible that God's Word is more valuable than gold or silver. Without the Bible, we could not know how to be saved from our sin.

WHEAT BOUQUETS

MATERIALS NEEDED PER CHILD

6-8 pieces of wheat (from craft store or wheat field)
1   piece of styrofoam 1½'' square
2   yards of ¾'' wide calico craft ribbon
1   chenille wire, 6'' long

GENERAL SUPPLIES NEEDED

Dried or silk flowers
Tacky glue
Pencil
Wire cutters

ADVANCE PREPARATION

Cut sheet of styrofoam into 1½'' blocks. Make bows. Make a sample of the craft.

DIRECTIONS

Bows:

Wrap 2 yards of ¾'' calico ribbon around a small book. Slide off and pinch in middle. Cut a small ''v'' shape from each side in the middle. Twist tightly with a 6'' piece of chenille wire. Pull out loops from bow and twist into place.

Craft:

Stick a pencil into the middle of the styrfoam block and pull the pencil all the way through to make a hole through the block. Slide 6-8 wheat stems through the hole in the styrofoam about half-way down the stems. If needed, glue in place with tacky glue. Use the chenille wires on the bow to fasten the bow in place over the styrofoam. Stick dried or silk flowers in the styrofoam around the bow. Glue when necessary. Set arrangement aside to dry.

CONVERSATION

Wheat, barley and other grains were very important in Bible days. Grain was one of the major foods then, just as it is today in many countries. [Apply specifically to the unselfishness of Ruth or the wisdom of Joseph, etc.]

FRUIT OF THE SPIRIT MOBILE

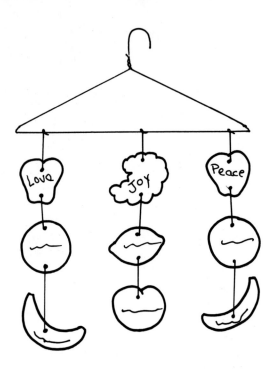

MATERIALS NEEDED PER CHILD

1   wire coat hanger, spray painted bright green

GENERAL SUPPLIES NEEDED

Construction paper, assorted colors
Poster patterns of fruit shapes (Pages 74-75)
Felt tip pens
String or thread
Paper punches
Invisible tape
Pencils
Scissors
Large sheets of newsprint
Masking tape

ADVANCE PREPARATION

Trace patterns onto poster board and cut out. Spray paint coat hangers. Make a sample.

DIRECTIONS

Trace 10 fruit shapes on different colors of construction paper. Write one fruit of the Spirit on each shape. Place a small piece of tape at the top of the fruit. Punch a hole through the tape and paper. Put a piece of tape at the bottom of 6 of the pieces of fruit and punch a hole through the tape and paper.

Use pieces of string or thread to tie the pieces together in two rows of 3 and one row of 4. Tie to coat hanger. Wrap a piece of tape around the coat hanger on each side of the thread to keep it from slipping out of place. Wrap your mobile in a sheet of newsprint and tape with masking tape. This will keep the threads from being tangled by the wind on the way home.

CONVERSATION

How can we tell if God's Spirit is in control of our lives? What happens when we sin? How can we have the fruit of the Spirit in our lives again after we have sinned? Can you have the fruit of the Spirit in your life if you are not a Christian? How can a person become a Christian?

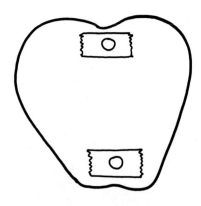

Place a piece of transparent tape on fruit before punching. Remember, 3 pieces of the fruit require only 1 hole.

REMINDER TO SPEAK LOVINGLY

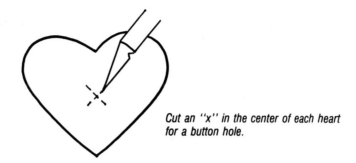

Cut an ''x'' in the center of each heart for a button hole.

MATERIALS NEEDED PER CHILD

1   4'' x 4'' piece of red construction paper
2   4'' x 4'' pieces of clear contact paper

GENERAL SUPPLIES NEEDED

Black, fine-point markers (Water Base)
Poster patterns of heart (Page 84)
Scissors
Pencils
X-acto knife for use by teacher only
Several layers of cardboard for teacher to cut on

ADVANCE PREPARATION

Trace heart pattern on poster board several times and cut out. Use X-acto knife to cut out holes in center of heart patterns. Cut construction paper and clear contact paper into 4'' squares. Make a sample.

DIRECTIONS

Trace the heart pattern on red construction paper. Draw a happy smile below the circle in the center. Draw happy eyes above the hole in the center. Ask your teacher to help you put contact paper on the front and back of your paper. Cut out the heart. Take it to the teacher and ask her to cut the button slits. Button the heart onto your shirt. If you don't have a button on the front, save it until you get home.

CONVERSATION

God wants us to think good thoughts and say kind and loving words. There is a prayer in the Bible that would be good for us to learn. It's found in Psalm 19:14. Let's read it from the Bible [read verse aloud]. These little hearts can remind us to pray and ask God to help us have good thoughts and say kind words. Let's listen to the verse again, then let's say the Bible verse together slowly with our heads bowed. We will pray the verse from the Bible, asking God to help us.

ANGEL

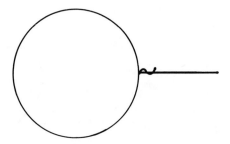

Bend wire to make a loop, leaving about 1'' at the end to insert in the styrofoam ball.

MATERIALS NEEDED PER CHILD

1   ½'' styrofoam ball
½   of a silver chenille wire
1   sheet of white card stock or construction paper
1   craft stick

GENERAL SUPPLIES NEEDED

Sequins
Tape
Glue
Silver glitter (optional)
Tacky glue

ADVANCE PREPARATION

Trace patterns onto poster board and make one set of patterns for each 5 children in your class. If you plan to use glitter, find a small, low box to keep the glitter from being wasted.

DIRECTIONS

Trace patterns onto white paper and cut out the shapes. Roll the angel body into a cone shape and tape it. Tape the wings to the back of the cone. Push one end of a craft stick into the styrofoam ball. Make a circle with your chenille wire, saving a little wire at one end to stick into the top of the styrofoam ball. Glue eyes and mouth onto the ball to make a face. Insert the craft stick into the top of the cone.

CONVERSATION

We don't really know what angels look like. But Mary and Joseph and the shepherds saw angels (Lk 2). How do you think they felt when the angels talked to them? What did the angels say to them?

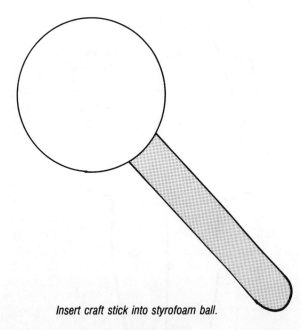

Insert craft stick into styrofoam ball.

Pattern for angel on page 94

POSTAGE STAMP CASE

MATERIALS NEEDED PER CHILD

1   Craft pattern xeroxed onto pastel card stock (page 89)
1   6'' x 8'' piece of contact paper
A few stickers

GENERAL SUPPLIES NEEDED

Scissors
X-acto knife (for teacher's use only)
Cardboard to protect table from knife

ADVANCE PREPARATION

Have craft pattern xeroxed onto cardstock (2 will fit on one sheet). Cut sheets in half. Cut contact paper to correct size. Cut apart stickers. Make a sample of the craft.

DIRECTIONS

Cut out craft on solid lines. Fold forward on all dotted lines. Fold in side flaps. Add stickers to front and back of case as desired. Place contact paper, clear side down on table. Carefully peel away backing. Unfold the craft, turn it sticker-side-down and press it onto the contact paper. Turn over and smooth out wrinkles. Ask teacher to cut a slit for the tab. [TEACHER: Work over cardboard to protect table surface.]

Trim contact paper even with all edges of the paper. Fold in the two side flaps, then fold up the bottom of the case. Use a 2¾'' strip of tape to tape each side by placing tape on table, sticky side up. Press case edge over half of the width of the tape, then fold over remaining tape to seal edges. Fold down top and slide tab into slot.

CONVERSATION

Have you ever started a job and then quit in the middle because you felt bored? Do you think it's good to be a quitter? If you give up on little jobs, will you ever learn to do big, important things? Who are some Bible people who finished the job God gave them to do? Can you think of any Bible people who quit too soon? What happened to them? What happens to people who stick to the job until it's finished? Did you know that's what a postage stamp does. It sticks to the envelope until the letter gets to where it is supposed to go. How would you feel if someone sent you a card and the stamp decided to quit before the card got to you? From now on, when you see a stamp on an envelope, think about how important it is to finish what you start. Make up your mind that you won't be a quitter.

49

10 PLAGUES TIME LINE

6-12 / 15 / L

GENERAL SUPPLIES NEEDED

10 large (12'' x 18'') sheets of manila paper
Crayons
Scissors
Scraps of assorted colors of construction paper
White art paper

ADVANCE PREPARATION

Letter one of the following titles at the top of each of the large sheets of manila paper:

BLOOD
FROGS
GNATS (NASB, NIV) or LICE (KJV)
INSECTS (NASB) OR FLIES (NIV, KJV)
CATTLE DIED
BOILS
HAIL
LOCUSTS
DARKNESS
FIRSTBORN DIED

DIRECTIONS

Work individually or in groups to illustrate one of the plagues. Be creative. Draw pictures or cut them from construction paper. If you like, make them 3-dimensional. When you finish, hang the illustrations in order.

CONVERSATION

Pharoah did not want to obey God. His heart was hard and rebellious (Ex 11). Have you ever felt that way about obeying your parents? How did Pharoah suffer for disobeying? How do we suffer when we disobey? What can we do when our hearts feel hard and we don't want to do what we are told — how can we make our hearts tender again?

50

CROSS BOOK MARK

GENERAL SUPPLIES NEEDED

Poster board patterns made from pattern on page 84
Glue
Pencils

MATERIALS NEEDED PER CHILD

1   5'' x 7'' piece of wallpaper
1   4½'' x 6'' piece of construction paper
1   flower sticker

ADVANCE PREPARATION

Trace and cut out several cross patterns. Cut wallpaper and construction paper to 4½'' x 6'' pieces to avoid waste. If stickers are on sheets, cut them apart.

DIRECTIONS

Trace cross pattern onto back of wallpaper and cut out. Trace cross pattern onto construction paper and cut out. Using your finger, rub white glue on the back of the wallpaper cross, filling in all the spaces. Place the construction paper cross on top and press down to seal in place. Write name on construction paper side. Turn cross over and put a sticker in the center of the cross.

CONVERSATION

The cross was a terrible thing. People were killed on crosses. But the cross is very special to people who believe in the Lord Jesus. It is like a valentine from God. Jesus showed how much He loved us when He died on the cross to wash away our sins. When your bookmark has dried, you can put it in your Bible to remind you of the wonderful love Jesus has for you.

PAINTED FLOWER POT

MATERIALS NEEDED PER CHILD

1   small clay flower pot

GENERAL SUPPLIES NEEDED

Tempera or acrylic paints
Clear nail polish
Small art brushes
Potting soil
Flower seeds — marigolds are easy to grow
Plastic bags with twist ties

ADVANCE PREPARATION

Make a sample of the craft.

DIRECTIONS

Paint ''God is Faithful'' around the rim of the flower pot. Paint flowers or other simple designs on the flower pot sides. Allow to dry overnight.

Paint lightly over the design and letters with clear nail polish. Fill the pot with soil and plant several seeds. Water lightly. Place in a plastic bag until you get home.

CONVERSATION

Sometimes it's hard to be patient, like when you're waiting for seeds to sprout and grow. But we mess things up when we try to rush something before God's perfect time. What Bible person learned the importance of being patient and waiting for God's timing?

When you take your flower pot home, set it in a sunny spot and water it lightly every day or two. Be patient and your plant will grow and flower.

Apply clear nail polish to protect design

FLUFFY LAMB PICTURE

MATERIALS NEEDED PER CHILD

1   xerox copy of lamb (page 71) on pastel card stock
1   bell
1   6'' piece of narrow ribbon or yarn
1   10mm wiggle eye
1   white felt ear
1   picture hanger (see page 6)

GENERAL SUPPLIES NEEDED

Cotton balls
Glue
Tape

ADVANCE PREPARATION

Xerox pattern on cardstock, one per child. Clip corners and fold forward on dotted lines, but do not tape. Cut ribbons and felt ears. Thread ribbon through bell and tie knot. Make a sample.

DIRECTIONS

Put your name on the back of the paper. Glue cotton balls to the lamb. Glue on an ear and eye. Glue ribbon around lambs neck, with bell hanging in front. Fold the edges of the picture forward and tape at the corners to make a frame. Tape a hanger on the back.

CONVERSATION

The Bible tells us a lot about sheep. What did today's story teach about sheep (Lk 15)? What does the story teach us to do? Why do you think God calls us His sheep?

Clip out corner pieces.

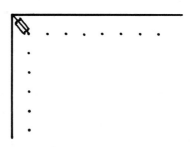

Fold up edges and tape at corners.

PENCIL CAN

MATERIALS NEEDED PER CHILD

1   aluminum can, washed and dried
1   piece of wallpaper, the same width as the can
1   piece of construction paper, the same width as the can
1   file folder with motto or short verse written on it

GENERAL SUPPLIES NEEDED

Glue
Tape
Stickers

ADVANCE PREPARATION

Cut construction paper and wallpaper to the correct size. Make a sample of the craft.

DIRECTIONS

Roll the construction paper and insert it into the can. If needed, glue in place. Put a line of glue around the top and bottom of the side of the can. Wrap the wallpaper around the can and fasten with tape to hold it until the glue dries. Decorate the can with stickers and stick on the Bible verse or motto.

CONVERSATION

Discuss today's story and how the motto or verse can help the child apply the truth of the story to his life.

SANDALS

MATERIALS NEEDED PER CHILD

1   square foot of vinyl
1   square foot of cardboard
2   30'' pieces of cord

GENERAL SUPPLIES NEEDED

Tacky glue
Scissors
Hole punch
Tape
Pencils

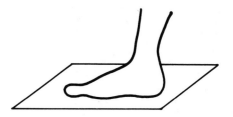

ADVANCE PREPARATION

Cut cardboard, vinyl and string into designated sizes, reserving some vinyl and cardboard in larger pieces — just in case. Make a sample.

DIRECTIONS

Trace your shoes on a piece of cardboard and cut out. Trace the sandal pattern on the back of the vinyl, adjusting the size by lengthening or shortening the heel and toe. Cut out the vinyl. Glue the cardboard to the wrong side of the vinyl. Punch holes in the sandal straps with a hole punch. Wrap a small piece of tape around each end of the cord to keep it from raveling. Use the cord to lace the sandal as shown. Cross the laces until the third strap. At the third strap, go straight to the fourth strap, bringing the lace around the heel and tying the laces in the front.

CONVERSATION

In Bible days, people did not have sewing machines and special materials to make sneakers and beautiful leather shoes. They made simple sandals from animal hides and tied them with leather laces. How do you think it felt to walk on hot, rocky roads with thin, flat sandals? Jesus loved people enough to walk from town to town to heal them and tell them about God. The disciples learned to love people too. You can find out what it felt like for the disciples. Put on your sandals when you get home and walk to a friend's house to tell him about Jesus. You can be a disciple and tell others about God's love.

Pattern for sandal on page 93

PAPER CLIP HOLDER

GENERAL SUPPLIES NEEDED

Glue
Sequins, lace, stickers
Felt tip pens

MATERIALS NEEDED PER CHILD

1   spray can lid
1   strip of magnetic tape to fit inside lid
1   file folder label
12 paper clips or hairpins

ADVANCE PREPARATION

Make a sample of the craft.

Peel strip from magnetic tape and stick magnet to inside of lid.

DIRECTIONS

Write the motto on a file folder label and stick it to outside of your up-side-down lid. Decorate the lid with stickers or sequins and lace. Attach the self-stick magnetic strip to the inside of the lid. Fill the lid with paper clips or hairpins.

SUGGESTED MOTTOS

Trust and Obey
Ready for God's Use
God Loves You
God Answers Prayer

CONVERSATION

Discuss how the chosen motto relates to the Bible story.

CRAYON RESIST

MATERIALS NEEDED PER CHILD

1   sheet of 9'' x 12'' white drawing paper

GENERAL SUPPLIES NEEDED

Black tempera, thinned with water
Large art brushes
Day-glo crayons
Newspaper

ADVANCE PREPARATION

Make a sample. Paper tables.

DIRECTIONS

Draw fireworks designs on your paper, pressing the crayons fairly hard, and going back over the lines to make them very bright. Use dots, straight, curved and zigzag lines.

Place newspaper under your drawing. Working quickly, brush black paint over your entire picture. Do not scrub the paint back and forth, just brush over each spot one time. Set aside your paper to dry.

CONVERSATION

Have you ever seen fireworks at night? The bright colors show up so well against the dark sky. A courageous person is like fireworks. When a person is brave in a dark and gloomy situation, his courage shows up like fireworks in a night sky. What are some dark and gloomy things you face? Maybe getting sick or maybe having it rain on the day of a picnic. When you are cheerful during those times, people will see your faith and your courage. You will look beautiful to others like the bright, sparkling fireworks.

PLASTIC CANVAS CROSS

MATERIALS NEEDED PER CHILD

1   canvas cross, color preferred
1   30'' piece of yarn
1   silk flower or flower sticker
1   darning needle

GENERAL SUPPLIES NEEDED

Tape
Extra yarn
Tacky glue

ADVANCE PREPARATION

Trace cross pattern on posterboard and cut out. Hold poster board cross over plastic canvas and cut out one cross per child. Cut yarn in 30'' lengths and fold a narrow piece of tape over ends as shown.

Pattern on page 75

DIRECTIONS

Tie a knot in the middle hole at top edge of the cross, leaving about 3'' of excess yarn [do not cut off excess]. Sew through each hole once, looping yarn around the outside. When you come to an outside corner, sew through it twice. Stitch all the way around cross, then stitch through the top, center hole one more time. Tie a knot. Trim the second end to a 3'' length.

For Necklace:

Measure a 24'' length of yarn and knot the ends together. Attach the cross to the center of the necklace, tying the 3'' lengths 3 times. Pull the knots tight. Trim the ends. Glue a flower at the center of the cross. Allow glue to dry before wearing.

For Bookmark:

Cut three 8'' lengths of yarn. Tie the two 3'' lengths of yarn attached to cross around the center of the 8'' strands, using several tight knots. Trim ends even. Stick on a flower sticker.

CONVERSATION

Have you ever wondered why Jesus had to die on the cross? Have you ever wished He had just stayed alive so He could be your Friend? What if Jesus had not died? Would we be able to wash away our sins and be forgiven? Would we be able to become God's children and have eternal life? Why not? We can be very thankful Jesus died on the cross and came back to life. We who believe in Him will see Him in Heaven someday.

SHARING BANK

MATERIALS NEEDED PER CHILD

1   cola can (pop top kind) washed and dried
1   strip of construction paper cut to size of can

GENERAL SUPPLIES NEEDED

Glue
Tape
Pencils
Pictures of world's children cut from magazine
Felt tip pens

DIRECTIONS

Put a band of glue around the top and bottom of the side of the cola can. Wrap paper around the can and tape in place until the glue dries. Cut out pictures of children's faces and glue them to the can. Use a felt tip pen to write, ''I will share with hungry people'' on the front of your bank. Take the bank home and save your pennies, then bring the money back to your teacher and ask her to send it to the poor people who need food.

CONVERSATION

The little boy in our story gave his lunch to Jesus (Jn 6). The boy was unselfish. When we give our pennies to Jesus, His helpers can use it to feed hungry people. How do you feel inside when you do something to help needy people? How do you think Jesus feels when you help the people He loves?

NOAH'S ARK MODEL

6-9 / 15 / M

GENERAL SUPPLIES NEEDED

Card stock or heavy construction paper
Crayons or markers
Scissors

MATERIALS NEEDED PER CHILD

4   spring-clip clothespins
4   wiggle eyes (optional)

ADVANCE PREPARATION

Make an ark by cutting a door and windows from a rectangular box. Paint with black tempera. Make a list of 4-legged animals to assign the children to make.

DIRECTIONS

Choose one of the animals from the teacher's list. Draw the shape of the animal's head and body (no legs) on paper and cut it out. Trace the shape and cut out a second animal. Glue one wiggle eye on each side of the head. Clip clothespins to the bottom of each animal to make legs. Stand your animals around the ark until it's time to go home.

CONVERSATION

God brought the animals two by two. Why did God send Noah and the animals into the ark (Gen 7)? Noah told other people about the flood, but the people did not believe. What happended to the people who did not believe and obey God? What should we learn from this story?

TO ADAPT FOR PRESCHOOL

Cut out animal shapes in advance. Allow children to color the animals, glue on wiggle eyes, and clip on clothespins.

FISH AND LOAVES RUBBINGS

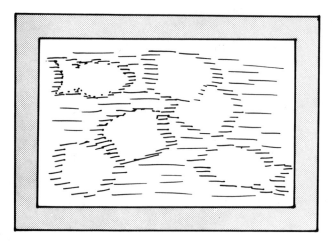

MATERIALS NEEDED PER CHILD

2   sheets of 9'' x 12'' construction paper
2   sheets of 8'' x 11'' typing paper

GENERAL SUPPLIES NEEDED

Scraps of construction paper
Craft glue
Crayons, unwrapped and clean
Patterns (page 77)

ADVANCE PREPARATION

Trace patterns onto poster board and cut out. Make several patterns each of the fish and loaves. Cut typing paper to 8'' x 11''. Make a sample craft. Since some blends of colors turn muddy, it's best to give the children only 3 colors. Blue, green and yellow work well. Red, orange and yellow also look good.

DIRECTIONS

Trace 5 loaves and 2 fish onto different colors of construction paper. Cut out the shapes and arrange on one sheet of white paper. Glue down and let glue dry. Place second sheet of white paper on top. Hold down tightly while you rub the side of a crayon over part or all of the picture. If you like, you may use several colors on top of each other, or next to each other. As you rub the crayon over the top sheet, the shapes of the fish and loaves will appear. Center each of the white sheets on a piece of construction paper. Glue in place.

CONVERSATION

Do you think the boy in the story of Jesus feeding 5,000 was hungry (Jn 6)? Was it easy for him to give his lunch to Jesus? What did Jesus do with the lunch? Did the little boy get enough to eat? How many baskets of food were left? How can you share with people who need food? What would you like to give to Jesus?

BOOKWORM HAIR CLIP

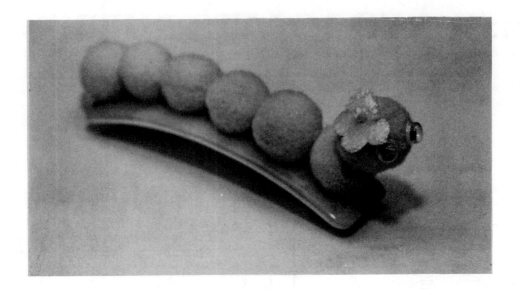

MATERIALS NEEDED PER CHILD

7-10   ½'' pom poms
1   barrette or clothespin
1   flexible magnet strip
2   4mm wiggle eyes
1   tiny silk flower

GENERAL SUPPLIES NEEDED

Craft glue

ADVANCE PREPARATION

Make a sample.

DIRECTIONS

Glue pom poms along the length of the barrette or clothespin. Allow to dry for a minute. Glue a pom pom to the top of one of the end pom poms. Glue two wiggle eyes and a flower to the caterpillar's head. Allow to dry before moving.

For Magnet:

When caterpillar is dry, stick a strip of flexible magnet to the other side of the clothesin.

CONVERSATION

Have you ever been called a bookworm? What does that nickname mean? What is the most important book for you to read? It's good for us to be Bible bookworms and to obey what we read in God's Word.

PATIENCE CHAIN

MATERIALS NEEDED PER CHILD

14 strips of construction paper 1'' x 9''
14 stickers
14 pieces of yarn, 10 inches long

GENERAL SUPPLIES NEEDED

Paper punches, 1 for every 4 children

ADVANCE PREPARATION

Cut paper strips on paper cutter. Cut yarn into 10'' lengths. Decide what the surprise will be at the end of two weeks — perhaps a party, special treat, prize for patient people, or puppet show. Make a sample.

DIRECTIONS

Fold paper around to form a loop with overlapping edges. Punch 2 holes in the overlapping part. Lace a piece of yarn through the 2 holes and tie a bow. Loop a second strip of paper through the first loop and punch through the overlapping ends. Lace with yarn and tie a bow. Repeat until all loops are used. Add a sticker to decorate each loop.

CONVERSATION

Is it hard for you to be patient? Most people don't like to wait, but it is important for us to learn to be patient. God knows when it is the right time for us to have what we want or need. If we don't wait for God's time, we will only cause problems for ourselves. Let's practice being patient for a special treat. In 2 weeks, that's 14 days, we will [explain the treat you've decided on]. You may take your patience chain home with you today. Each day, before you go to bed, you may untie 1 loop. Save the loop of the yarn in case you want to make the patience chain again for something else. Each day, the chain will get shorter. Each day, ask God to help you learn to be patient, knowing that when it is the right time, God will bless you with special things. After you open up the last loop on your chain, you can go to bed knowing you will have a special treat when you come to class the next morning.

TEACHER: Take your patience chain home and remove loops as a reminder of how many days you have to prepare the treat for the children. Don't let it become a procrastination chain, though!

EGGSHELL FISH

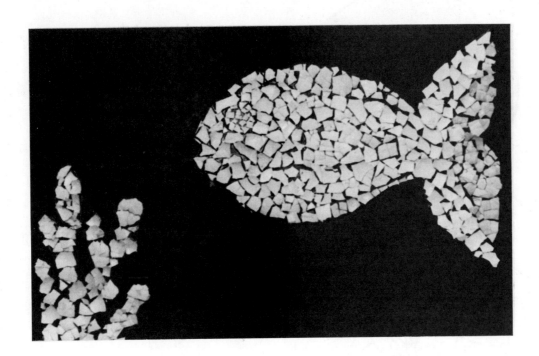

MATERIALS NEEDED PER CHILD

¼ sheet of black, blue, or white posterboard

GENERAL SUPPLIES NEEDED

White glue
Colored egg shell pieces
Pencils
Patterns (optional, page 86)
Netting from fabric department (⅔ yard will be plenty)
Old cups or bowls
Plastic spoons
Newspapers
Paper towels
Baggies

ADVANCE PREPARATION

Xerox pattern for each child if desired. Save and wash eggshells, peeling out the thin membrane on the inside of the egg. When you've collected 4-5 eggshells per child, break them into ½'' pieces. To dye, mix Easter egg dye (or the recipe on food coloring box) in old cups or bowls. Divide eggshells and place in center of 12'' square netting. Gather the corners of the net, and submerge eggshells in dye. Stir occasionally with plastic spoon to be sure all shells are colored. When shells reach desired color, gather corners of net and lift out shells. Spread paper towels over newpaper pads. Spread shells over paper towels to dry, keeping colors separate. When shells are completely dry, place in plastic bags, and use twist ties to close. Cut poster boards in fourths. Make a sample.

DIRECTIONS

Draw a fish or transfer pattern to poster by placing on top of poster board and pressing hard over all the lines to make an indentation on the poster. Remove pattern and darken lines on poster with a pencil, if you like. Fill one area of the fish at a time with a layer of glue, then press in the shells you like. Put the shells close together, but leave a little of the poster showing around the shells. Fill in the entire fish, one color at a time. If you want, add bubbles or water plants.

CONVERSATION

What does your daddy do for a living? Do you know what Peter did for a living (Lk 5)? Sometimes Peter fished and fished but did not catch anything. How do you think he felt when he worked hard but did not come home with any fish to sell? What happened when Jesus told Peter where to throw his nets? How did Jesus know Peter would catch a lot of fish?

WORSHIP SILHOUETTE

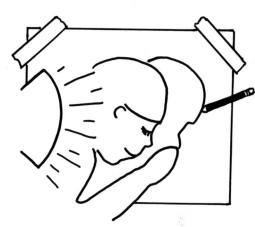

Seat child between light and paper. Trace outline.

MATERIALS NEEDED PER CHILD

1   sheet light blue or light pink construction paper (12'' x 18'')
1   sheet black construction paper (12'' x 18'')

GENERAL SUPPLIES NEEDED

Clamp lamp with reflector (available at discount or hardware stores)
White or yellow colored pencil
Scissors
Glue stick
Flair pens

ADVANCE PREPARATION

Make a sample of the craft. Set up an area with a chair against a smooth wall and a place to clamp the lamp. Move lamp and chair until you get a sharp outline of a child sitting in the chair (child should be close to the wall, lamp about 18'' away). A dark area is best. You will need 1 or 2 people to trace the outlines of the children while you keep the others busy.

DIRECTIONS

TEACHER: Tape a sheet of black construction paper on the wall beside the child, who should face forward. Have child bow head, close eyes and hold up ''praying hands.'' Trace the outline of the child's head, arms and hands. To avoid restless children, trace one child at a time during recess, refreshments or workbook time — or provide paper for coloring until silhouettes are finished.

Child will cut out silhouette carefully on the pencil line and will apply gluestick to the silhouette and glue it to light blue or light pink paper. Then use a flair pen to write the words, ''I Will Worship the Lord,'' and/or a short Bible verse.

CONVERSATION

What does it mean to worship the Lord? Have you ever taken time to think about how great our God is? The Lord deserves our respect and our love and our praise. Let's think of several ways to worship the Lord at home and at church.

OPTION: If you wish to make a more permanent craft, obtain a piece of wood 12'' x 18''. Allow children to paint it with latex paint (protect clothing with men's old shirts, buttoned in the back). When paint is dry, children may brush a mixture of white glue and water over the board and carefully place their silhouette in position. Then they may brush on another coat of glue mixture. Children may add as many coats as they wish, but they must allow glue to dry thoroughly between coats. The verse may be written in permanent ink on construction paper and decoupaged beside or below the silhouette.

CLOTHESPIN WELL

MATERIALS NEEDED PER CHILD

11 clothespins (spring clip type) pulled apart
1   4¼ ounce baby food jar, washed and dried
1   adhesive label for child's name
20'' colorful yarn
1   small plant

GENERAL SUPPLIES NEEDED

Tacky glue
Potting soil
Pen
Small bags

ADVANCE PREPARATION

Pull apart clothespins and count 21 halves for each child and place in bags. Make a sample craft.

DIRECTIONS

First day:

Write your name on label and stick to bottom of baby food jar. With finger, coat sides of jar with glue. Glue clothespins to jar, flat side in, clip end pointed upward. It takes 17 to go around the jar. Secure the pins with yarn, tied around the small notch in the centers of the clothespins. Glue 2 of the clothespins on opposite sides of the well, flat side out, matching notches on clip ends. Hold in place until dry enough to stick.

Second day:

Use paper, made into a cone funnel, to fill jar with potting soil. Plant flower. Add final clips to well, resting flat side notches on the points of the 2 standing clips. Glue in place.

CONVERSATION

Without water, people could not live very long. That's why the people in Bible days dug wells in their towns. They would lower buckets into the well to get water for cooking and drinking. Have you ever been very, very thirsty? How does it feel? Can you think about anything else when you are thirsty? The Bible tells us to be thirsty for God. What do you think that means? Do you remember a story about a woman who came to a well for water and found out that she was really thirsty to know God?

FAVORITE FOODS POSTER

MATERIALS NEEDED PER CHILD

¼   sheet of colored poster board
1   colorful paper plate
1   plastic knife
1   plastic fork
1   plastic spoon
1   memory verse card
1   white paper triangle the size of a napkin

GENERAL SUPPLIES NEEDED

Magazine pictures of food
White glue
Crayons

ADVANCE PREPARATION

Cut posters and paper napkins. Tear out magazine pictures of food. Make a sample of the craft. Make a memory verse card for each student.

DIRECTIONS

Cut out pictures of food and glue them to the plate. Arrange the plate, utensils, napkin and verse card on the poster. Glue down the napkin first, then the plate. Glue the utensils in place, then the memory verse card. Use crayons to decorate the corners of the placemat and to write your name on your craft.

CONVERSATION

Did Daniel complain and fuss about the food he was given (Dan 1)? How did he ask for other food? Did Daniel ask selfishly for foods he liked, or did he ask for foods that would please God? Which boys grew the strongest — the ones who ate all the meats and sweets or the ones who ate the vegetables? What should you do when someone offers you something your parents would not want you to eat? Will God bless you for doing what is right?

MAP PLAQUE

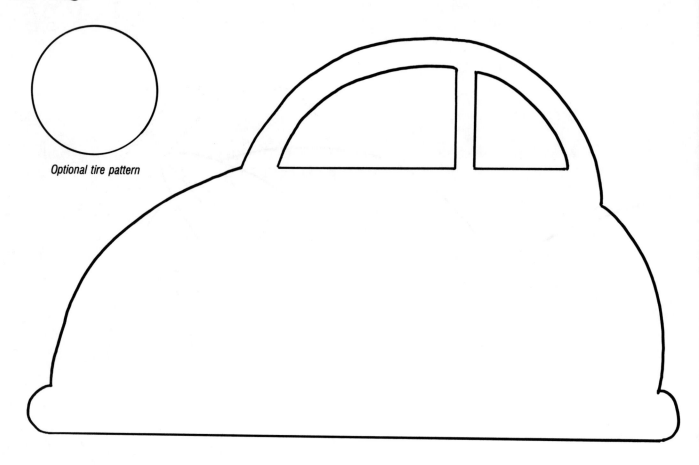

Optional tire pattern

LION'S FACE

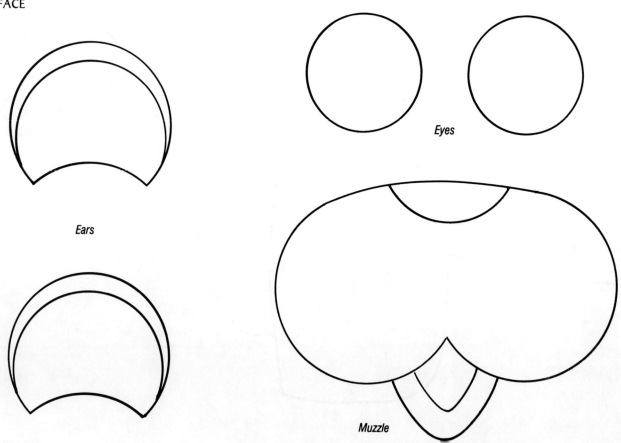

Ears

Eyes

Muzzle

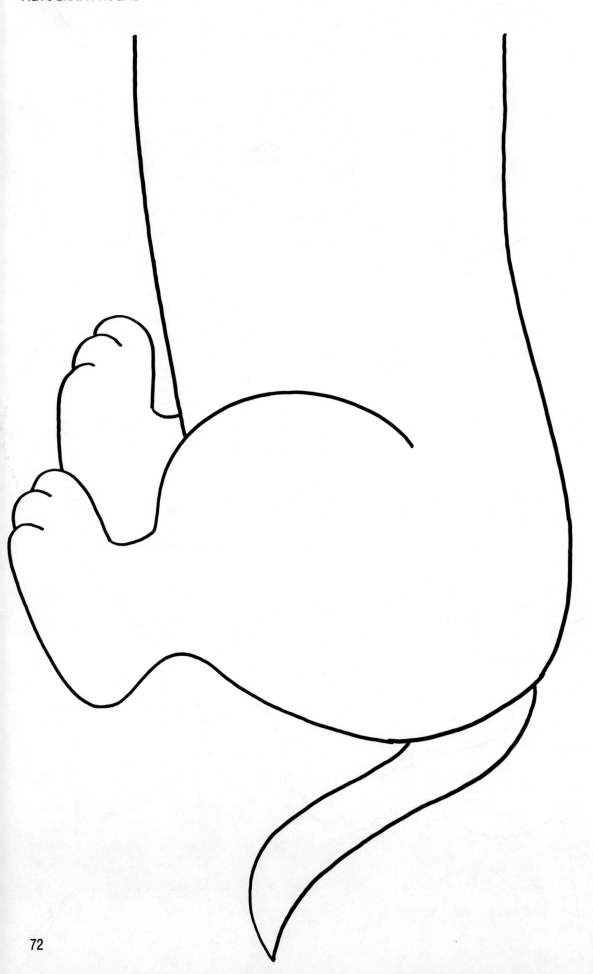

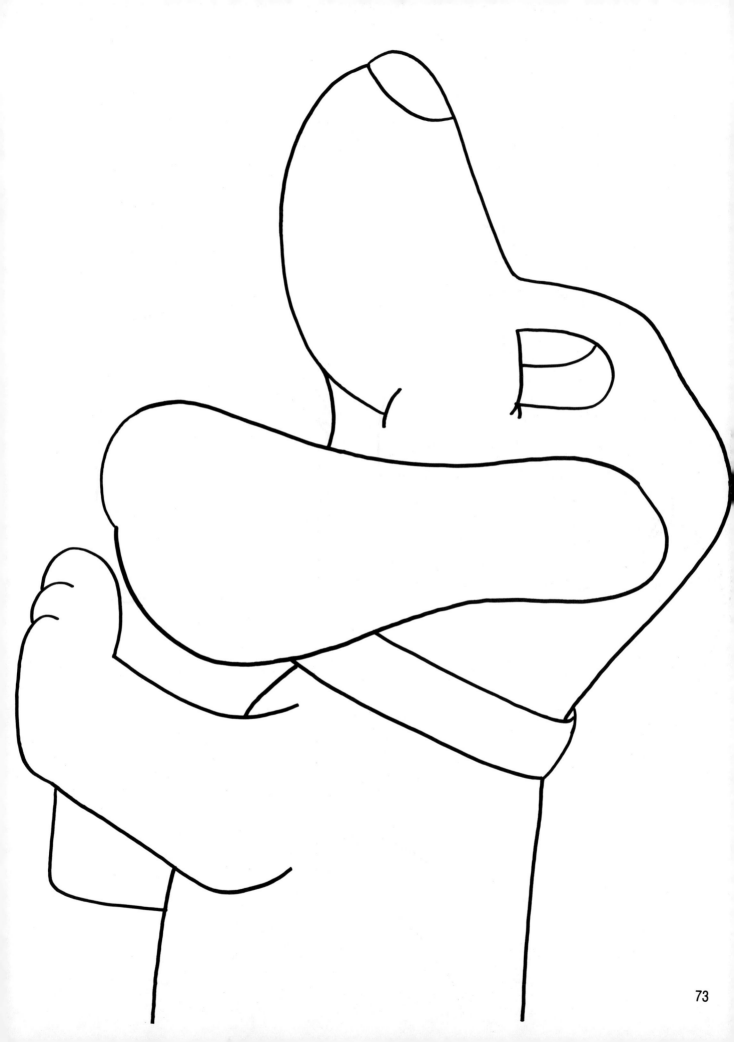

73

FRUIT OF THE SPIRIT MOBILE

SPIDER WEB STRINGING TOY

Spider body

LION SOCK BANK

PLASTIC CANVAS CROSS

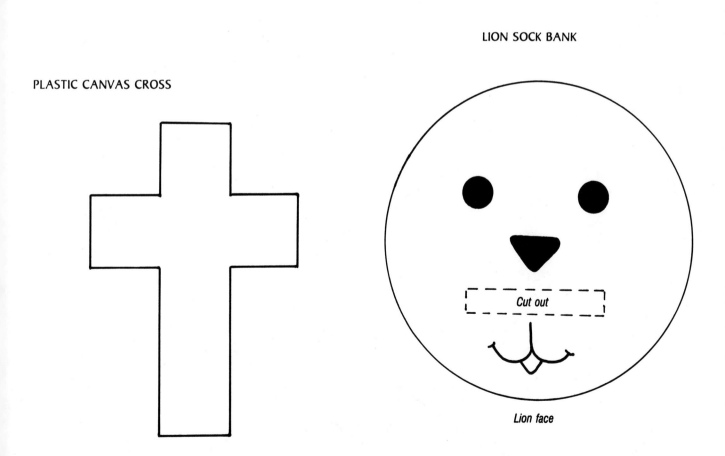

Cut out

Lion face

Thy word I have
treasured in my heart,
That I may not sin
against Thee.

Psalm 119:11

T-SHIRT

FISH AND LOAVES RUBBINGS

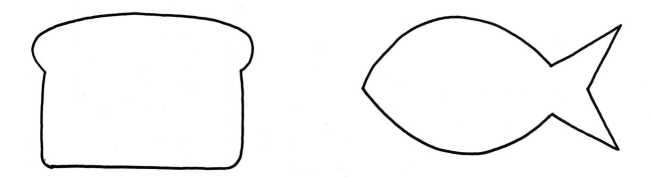

Rejoice in the Lord !

JESUS DESK PLAQUE

GOSPEL STORY BOARD

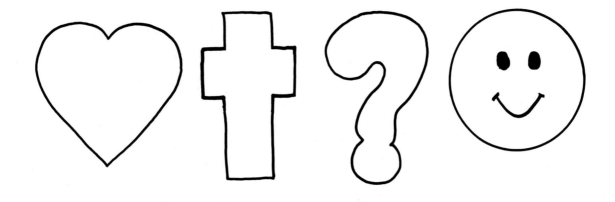

RAINBOW MOBILE

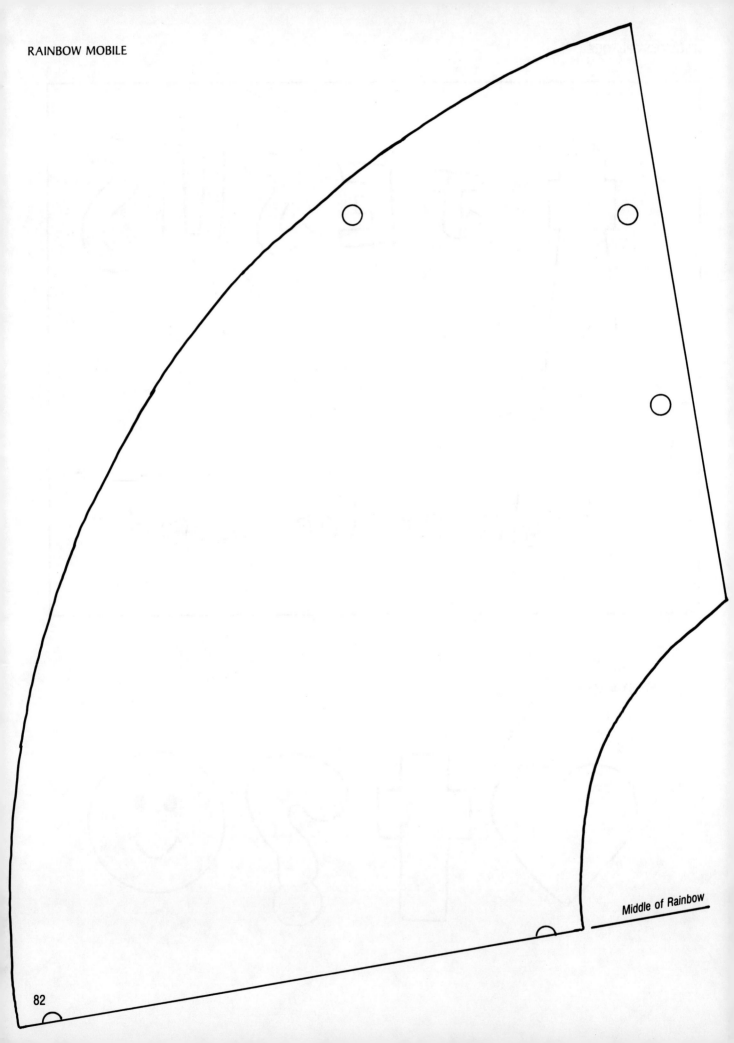

Middle of Rainbow

82

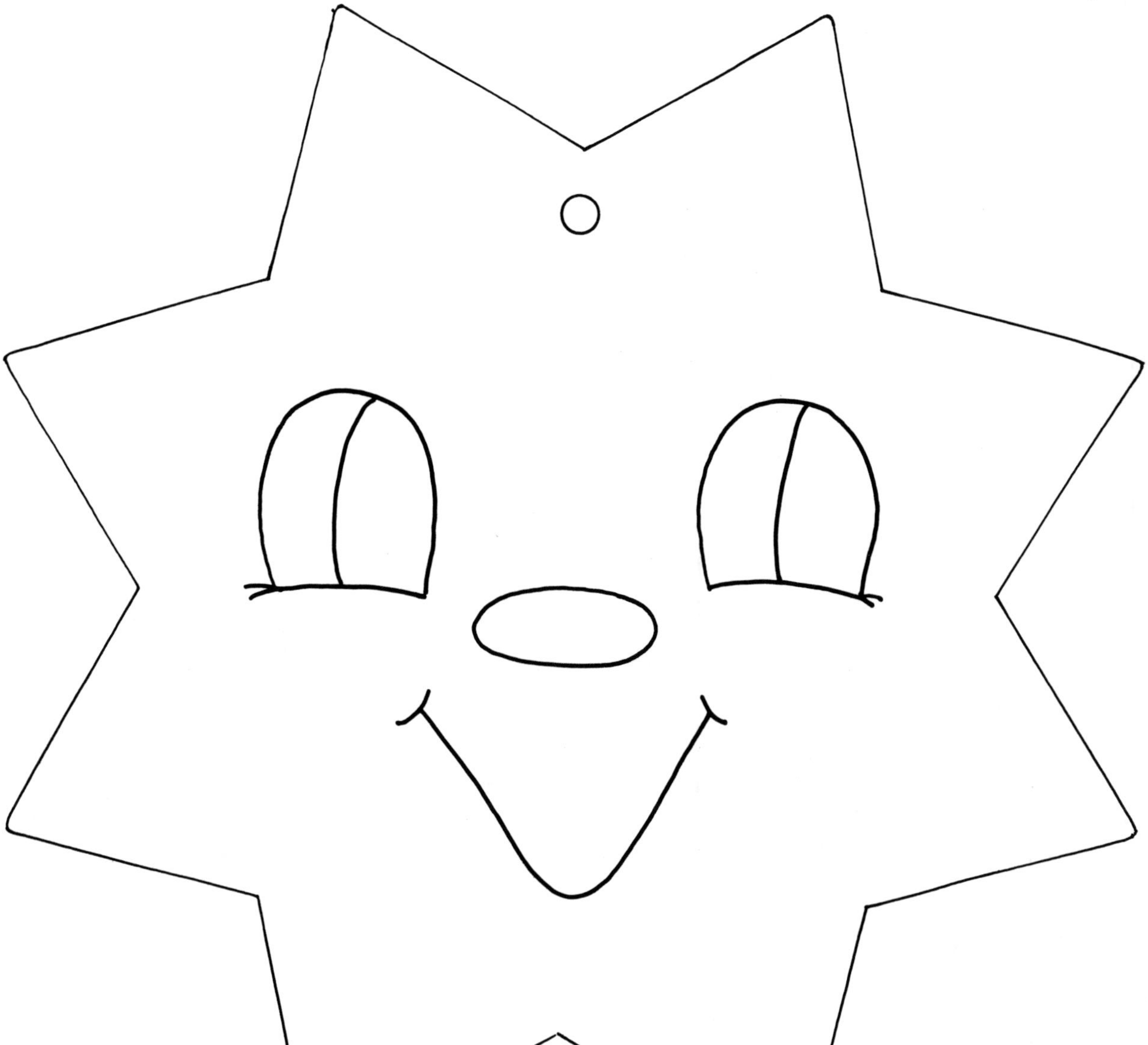

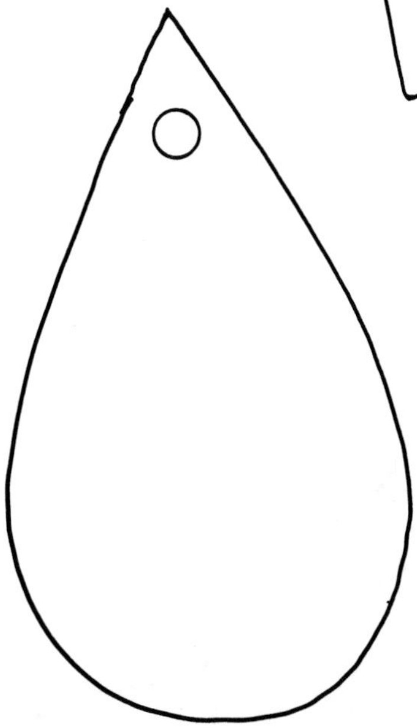

CROSS BOOK MARK

MEMORY VERSE STRINGER

REMINDER TO SPEAK LOVINGLY

84

JOY BREAD DOUGH PLAQUE

MANY-LAYERED KEY CHAIN

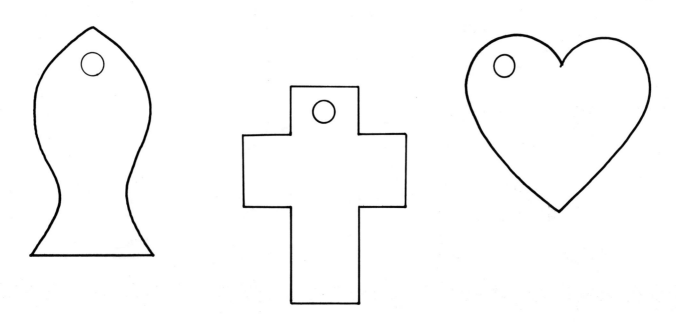

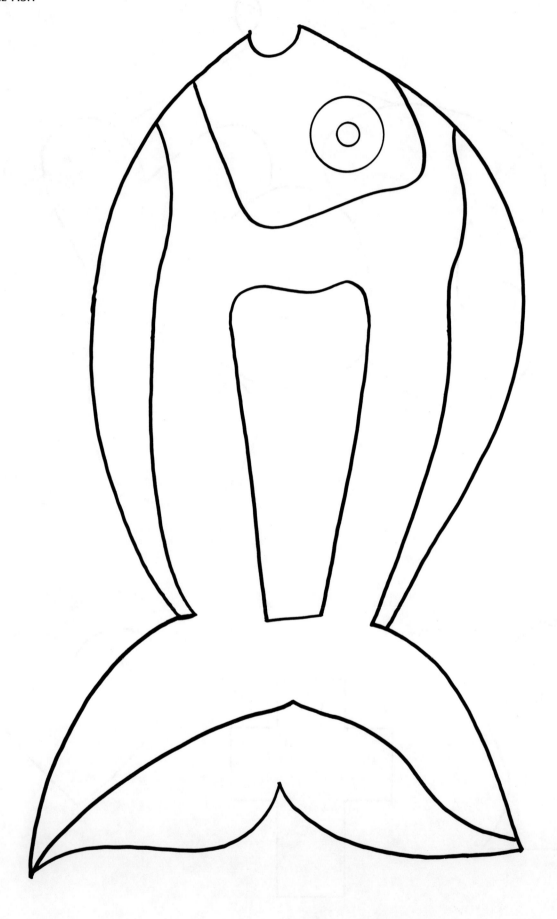

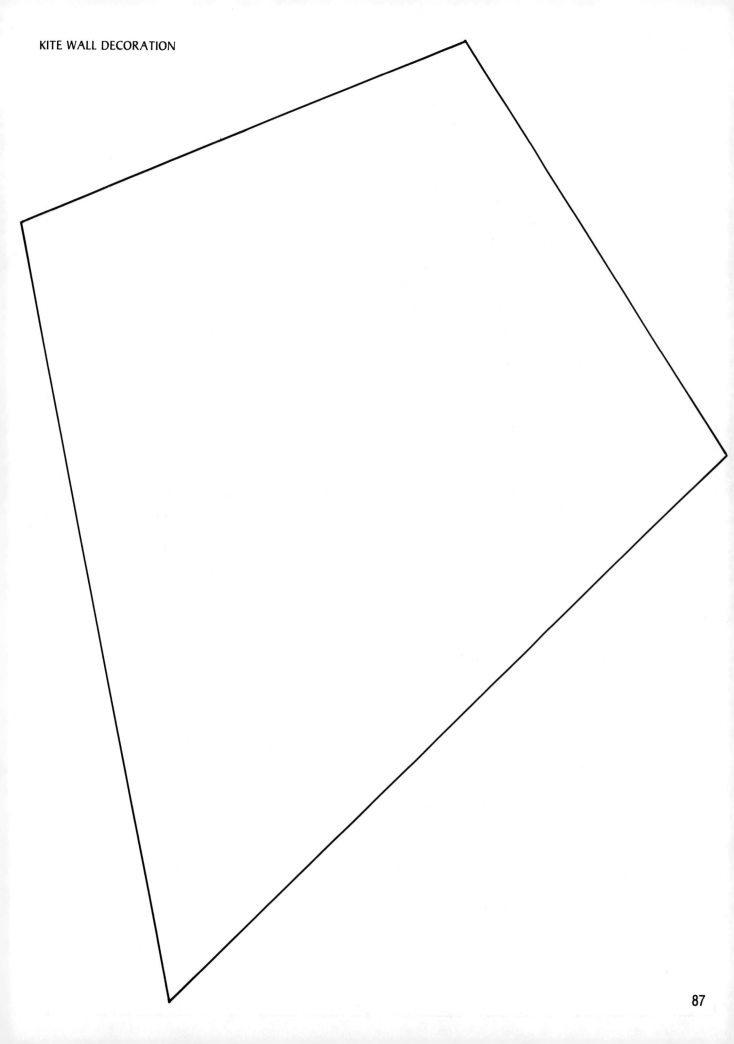

POSTAGE STAMP CASE

Until it's Done!

Stick to the Job

89

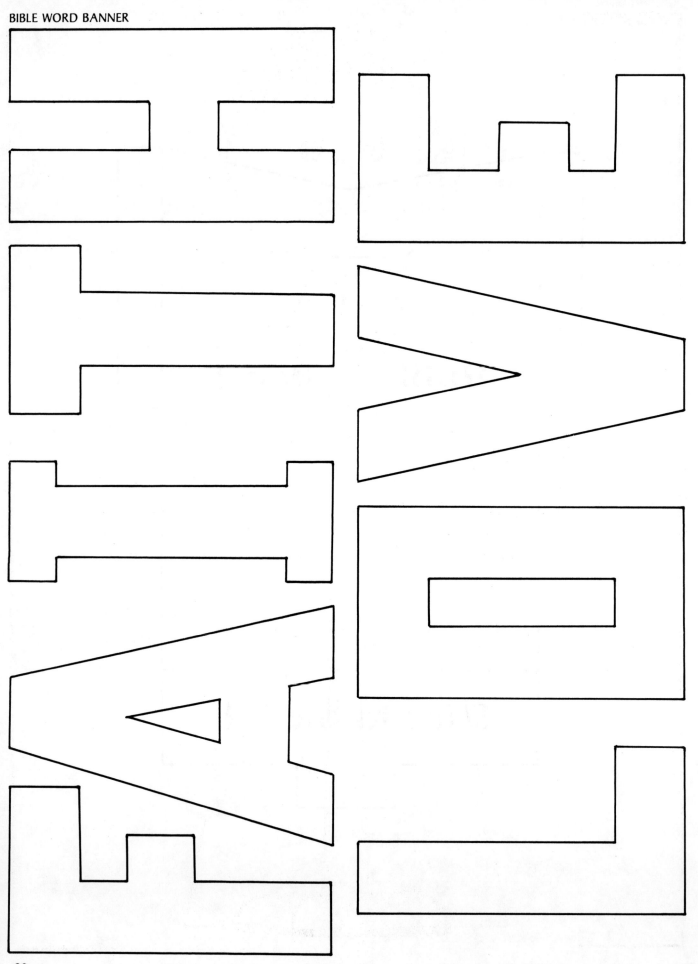

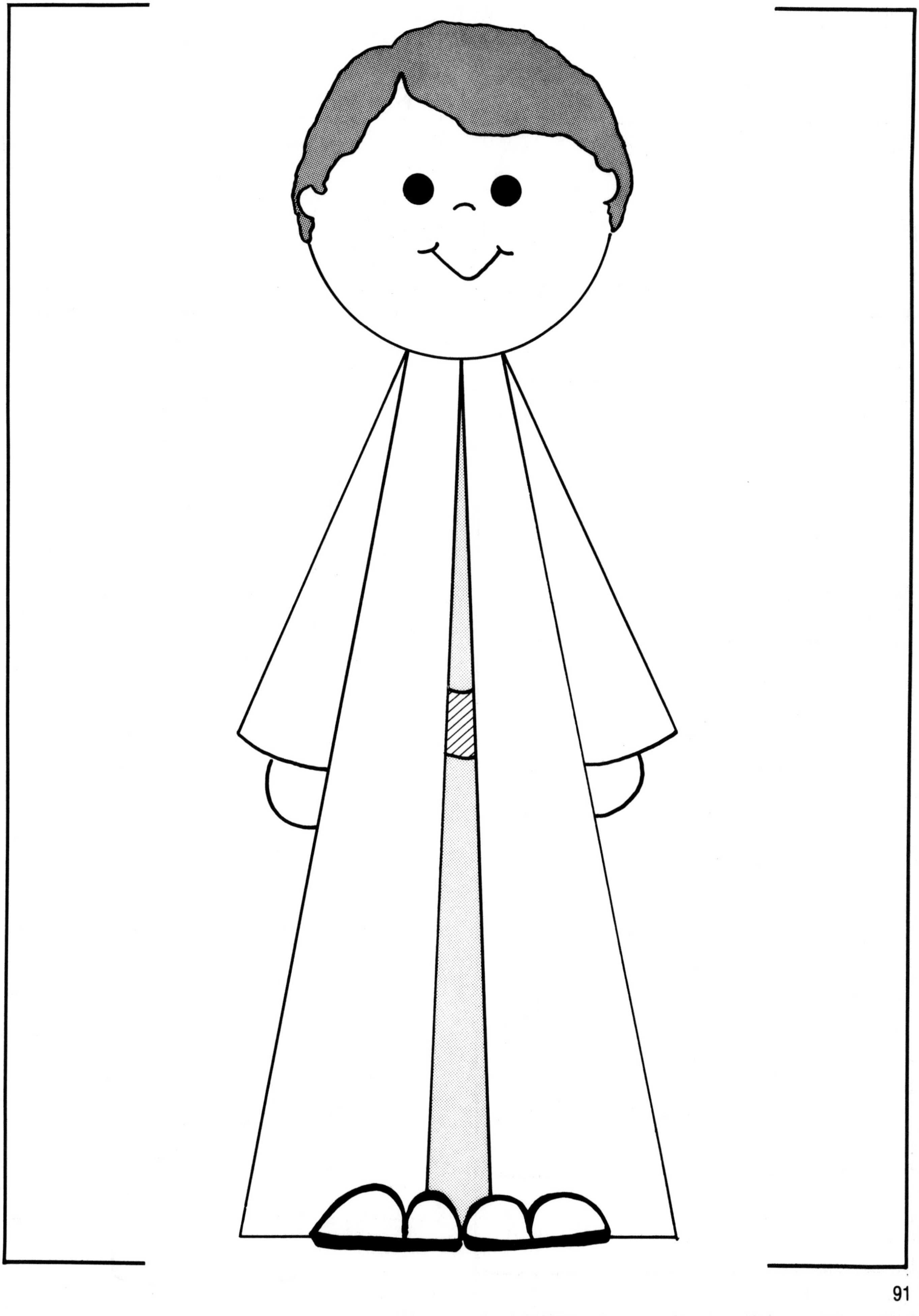

DOOR KNOB HANGER   PAPER TRUMPET

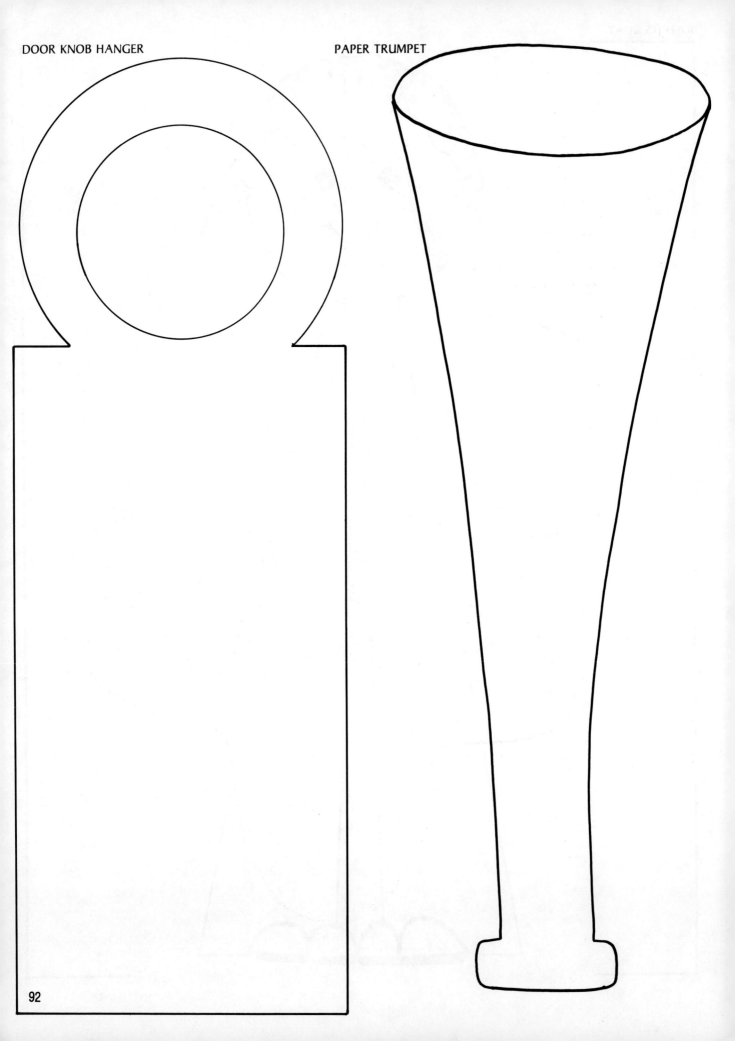

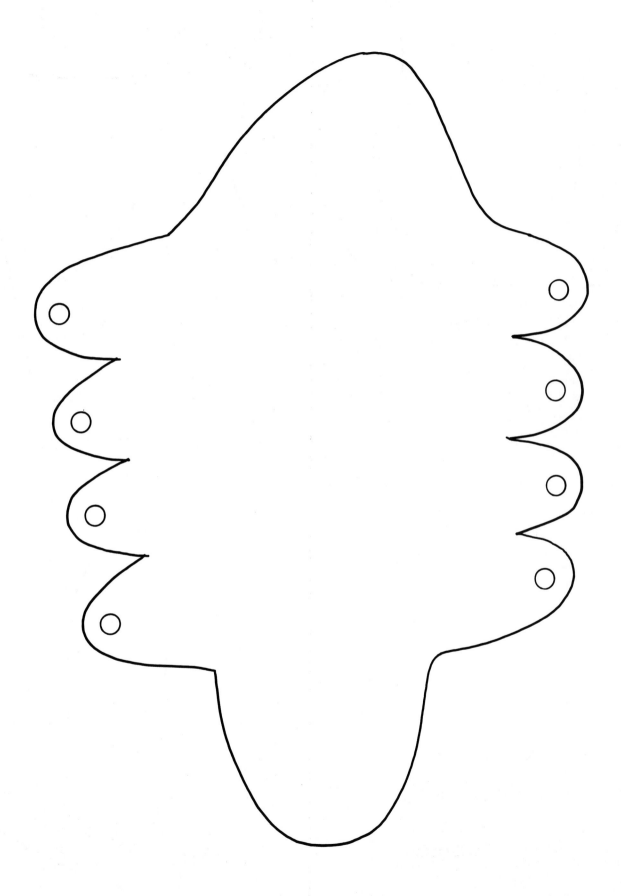

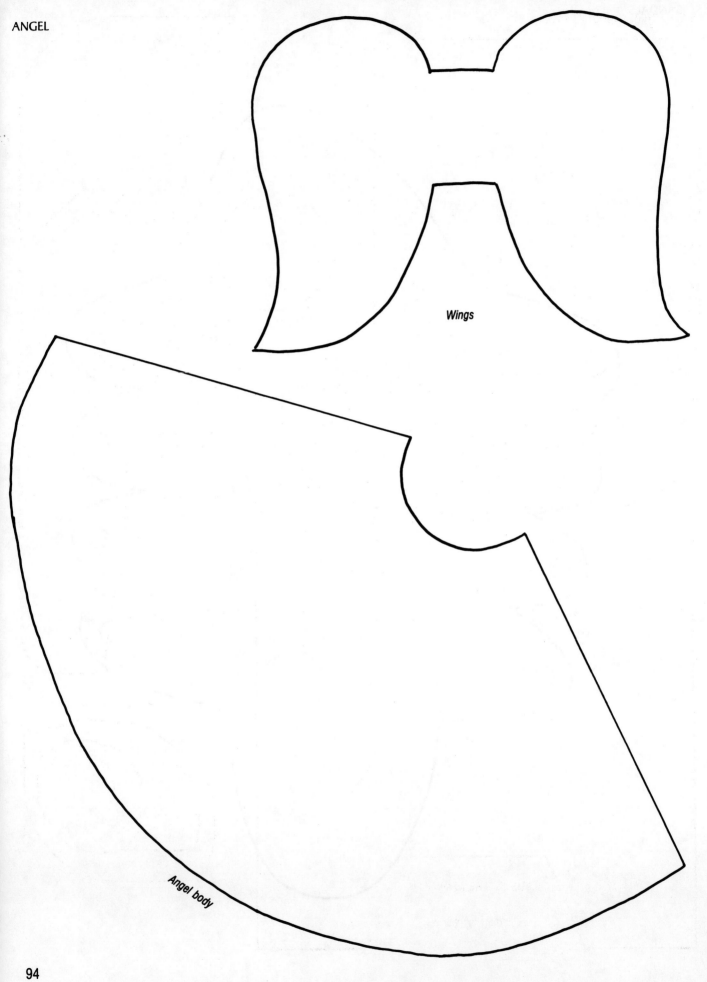

Wings

Angel body

SIN

JESUS IN THE MANGER

End for manger